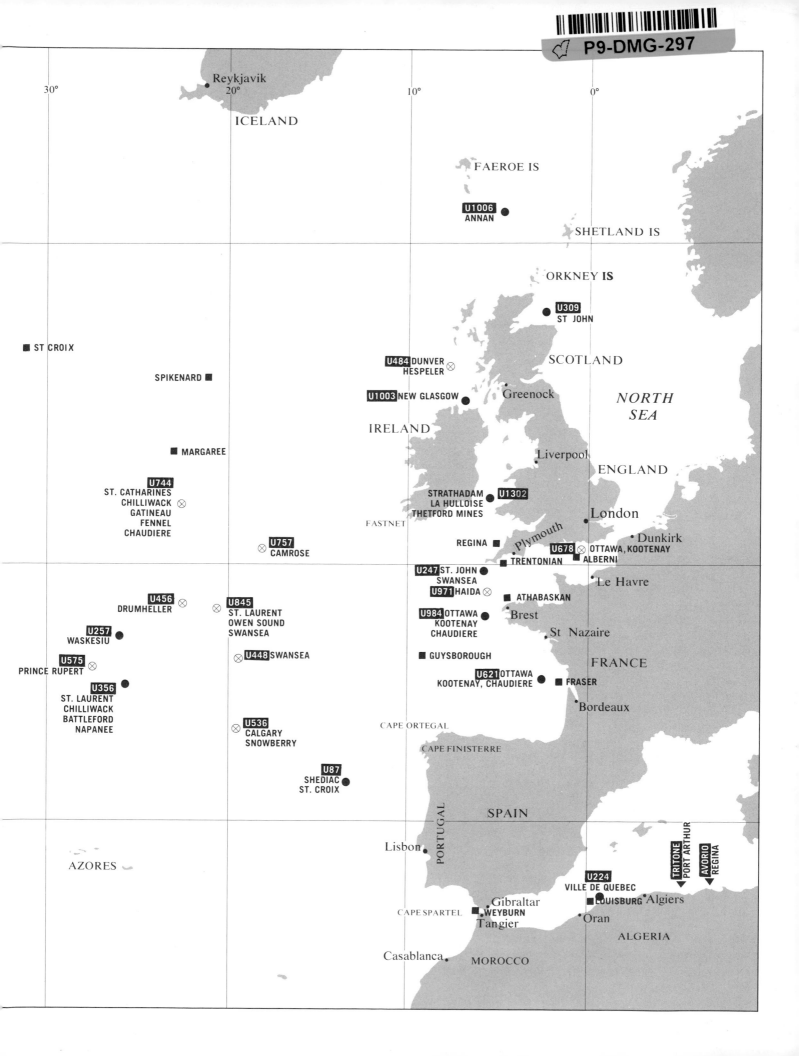

30°   20°   10°   0°

Reykjavik

ICELAND

FAEROE IS

U1006 ANNAN

SHETLAND IS

ORKNEY IS

U309 ST JOHN

SCOTLAND

NORTH SEA

ST CROIX

U484 DUNVER HESPELER ⊗

SPIKENARD ■

U1003 NEW GLASGOW ●   Greenock

IRELAND

Liverpool   ENGLAND

MARGAREE ■

U744 ST. CATHARINES CHILLIWACK GATINEAU FENNEL CHAUDIERE ⊗

STRATHADAM   U1302
LA HULLOISE
THETFORD MINES

London

FASTNET

Plymouth   Dunkirk

REGINA ■   U678 ⊗ OTTAWA, KOOTENAY

U757 CAMROSE ⊗

TRENTONIAN ■   ALBERNI

U247 ST. JOHN ●
SWANSEA

Le Havre

U456 DRUMHELLER ⊗   U845 ST. LAURENT OWEN SOUND SWANSEA

U971 HAIDA ⊗
ATHABASKAN ■

U257 WASKESIU ●

U984 OTTAWA ●
KOOTENAY
CHAUDIERE   Brest

U575 PRINCE RUPERT ⊗   U448 SWANSEA ⊗

St Nazaire

U356 ●
ST. LAURENT
CHILLIWACK
BATTLEFORD
NAPANEE

GUYSBOROUGH ■

FRANCE

U621 OTTAWA ●
KOOTENAY, CHAUDIERE   FRASER ■

U536 CALGARY SNOWBERRY ⊗

Bordeaux

CAPE ORTEGAL

CAPE FINISTERRE

U87 SHEDIAC ● ST. CROIX

SPAIN

AZORES

PORTUGAL

Lisbon

TRITONE PORT ARTHUR ▼

AVORIO REGINA ▼

U224 VILLE DE QUEBEC

CAPE SPARTEL   Gibraltar   LOUISBURG ■   Algiers
WEYBURN ■
Tangier   Oran

Casablanca   MOROCCO   ALGERIA

Canada's Atlantic War

Canada's Atlantic War

Text by
John Swettenham

Illustrations by
Fred Gaffen

Samuel-Stevens
Toronto & Sarasota
1979

Samuel-Stevens Edition (Canada)
ISBN 0-88866-604-7

Samuel Stevens Edition (U.S.)
ISBN 0-89522-018-0

Canadian Cataloguing in Publication Data

Swettenham, John, 1920-
  Canada's Atlantic war

Bibliography: p.
Includes index.
ISBN 0-88866-604-7

1. World War, 1939-1645 — Atlantic Ocean.
2. World War, 1939-1945 — Naval operations,
Canadian. I. Gaffen, Fred. II. Title.

D770.S85   940.54'21   C79-094262-3

Design by Maher & Murtagh

Printed and bound in Canada

Samuel-Stevens, Publishers, Ltd.
554 Spadina Crescent
Toronto, Ontario M5S 2J9

Samuel Stevens and Company
P.O. Box 3899
Sarasota, Florida 33578

Photograph Credits
Numbers refer to plate numbers.
Australian War Memorial: 113. Bethlehem Steel Corporation: 132.
Bognasco, Erminio: 110, 126, 176, 208. British Information Services:
2. Bundesarchiv: 6, 10, 11, 12, 13, 14, 16, 18, 32, 37, 66, 67, 115,
143, 150, 169, 180, 205, 211, 214. Canadian War Museum: 21, 31,
64, 144, 150, 166, 192. Czechoslovak Military Museum: 3.
Department of National Defence: 202. Dobson, Mrs. A. H.: 165.
Franklin D. Roosevelt Library: 94, 151. Frère-Cook, G.: 130. Her
Majesty's Stationery Office: 4, 5, 19, 20, 26, 27, 34, 38, 39, 40, 41,
44, 45, 62, 147, 168, 188. Imperial War Museum: 7, 10, 15, 17, 22,
47, 48, 50, 53, 59, 68, 70, 76, 80, 92, 99, 102, 107, 108, 109, 112,
114, 118, 121, 122, 123, 128, 136, 138, 139, 140, 142, 148, 149, 151,
152, 154, 155, 156, 163, 164, 171, 172, 173, 174, 175, 177, 178, 179,
181, 183, 188, 189, 190, 191, 195, 209, 210, 213, 215, 217, 218, 219,
221, 229, 231, 232. Keeley, M.G.C./A.J. Watts Collection: 119.
Murwik Naval College (W. Germany): 116. Musée de la Marine, Paris:
36. National Library of Canada: 42. National Maritime Museum,
Antwerp: 23, 24. Norwegian Official: 98. Public Archives Canada: 25,
28, 30, 43, 46, 51, 52, 54, 55, 56, 57, 58, 60, 61, 63, 71, 75, 77, 78,
79, 84, 85, 87, 91, 93, 96, 104, 120, 124, 131, 134, 135, 137, 162,
167, 170, 185, 186, 187, 194, 196, 197, 199, 201, 204, 206, 207, 208,
212, 220, 222, 223, 224, 225, 226, 227, 228, 230. Public Records
Office: 157, 158. Pugsley, W.H.: 73, 74, 81, 82, 83, 86, 88, 89, 105,
200. Salamander Books: 161. Stato Maggiore della Marina, Rome: 35,
111, 125, 146. Stephenson, Sir William: 95. Sun Oil Company: 145.
The Times: 33. United States Army: 97. United States National
Archives: 8, 9, 29, 49, 72, 100, 101, 103, 127, 133, 146, 153, 164,
184, 192, 198, 203. United States Navy: 65, 69, 141, 159, 160, 193.
Weir, Godfrey: *PQ-17*, London: Hutchinson & Co., 1946: 106.
Zeitgeschichtliches Bildarchiv: 129. Special thanks to the staffs of the
following institutions:
  Bundesarchiv, Canadian Forces Directorate of History, Her
Majesty's Stationery Office and the Public Archives of Canada.
  The photographs of Dr. W.H. Pugsley, the assistance of John Griffin
and Ken Macpherson, and the technical assistance of E&K
Productions, are gratefully acknowledged.

Contents

Foreword

I am honoured by John Swettenham to have been asked to write a foreword for this excellent and timely book on the Battle of the Atlantic, the longest campaign of the Second World War. We Canadians took on a large share of the struggle to keep the sea-lines open throughout six years of war.

It is only now, more than three decades since the war ended, that it has been possible to release enough information to the public domain for historians to be able to put the Battle into its true context in the Second World War, and, perhaps more importantly, to start assessing all the factors involved in its conduct on both sides. This is the first Canadian book to give a brief *overall* naval story; including the degree of preparedness of the contestants, their plans, their fortunes throughout the years, the rival technologies, the influence of air power, the political background, how ''Ultra'' contributed (through the decrypting of German signals), the effect that land operations had on those by sea; and the influence of industrial production in the shipyards, and of agriculture on the farms. Such a book cannot deal with Canada in a vacuum. It must place the Canadian effort into the context of what the British were doing, and the Americans, and it must describe the complexities which arose in the Mediterranean and the Arctic, as well as in Atlantic waters. Nor can it ignore the merchant marine — whether of Canada, Britain, or other belligerent (or even neutral) nations — on whose courage and determination the outcome, in the final analysis, depended.

Although we have an official account of the activities of the Royal Canadian Navy ashore during the Second World War, there is no similar work which has focussed on the *overall* part of the Royal Canadian Navy. There is of course Joseph Schull's fine book, *The Far Distant Ships*, which has been the closest thing we have had to a history of Canada's part at sea. There have been other books, mostly personal reminiscences, but they are few and limited in scope.

I have never been in a battle, thanks to the efforts of those who fought in the war and those who have led us in the peace which we have enjoyed. There are precious few serving naval officers who have been in a sea battle, in any navy. Although conditions are vastly different today from what they were in the war, there are profound lessons to be learned from history, and without personal experience, naval planners must turn to historians to help them in their tasks. This places an added burden on historians to make sure their work is accurate.

The Second World War obviously stirs a great deal of interest among those who took part, but it also arouses great interest among younger people who are anxious to learn what really happened. It seems to me that John Swettenham has produced a book which can go a long way towards satisfying their curiosity. It is comprehensive, lucid, and puts the campaign in context. With Fred Gaffen's more than two hundred illustrations, which fit the text remarkably, we have here an account in word and picture of a crucial sea campaign that gives a clear view of its grimness as well as its importance.

The Atlantic bridge is still the structure on which Western security and defence depends, and this book is a timely reminder to us all.

Rear-Admiral
Chief Maritime Doctrine and Operations

Preface

This is a short account of the Battle of the Atlantic, 1939-1945, an epic struggle of the Second World War.

It is not particularly intended for specialists or other experts. My aim is to provide an outline of what the Atlantic lifeline meant, and how it survived, for members of the present generation — particularly for those at school. The book is an attempt to pull together many facets, each of which has been the subject of many books, and to give a clear picture of the overall battle and Canada's part in it.

I am grateful to Rear-Admiral Mainguy, who read the text and commented on it; and especially for his foreword. My thanks also to two other readers — Lee Murray of the Canadian War Museum, himself a sailor, and Dr. W.E. Taylor, Director of the National Museum of Man. Barbara MacDonald typed the many drafts with patience and proficiency. The work of my colleague, Fred Gaffen, needs no acknowledgement — the illustrations speak for themselves.

For assistance with research, and other materials, Fred and I are indebted to Mr. William Constable of the Canadian Forces Directorate of History; to John Griffin; and to W.H. Pugsley.

A very special debt is owed to the Ontario Arts Council which has very generously supported the work throughout.

The responsibility for opinions expressed, and for the accuracy or inaccuracy of the statements made, rests with me.

J.A.S.

1. *Blitzkrieg* in Poland.

Introduction

Introduction

At 11:15 A.M. on 3 September 1939 Prime Minister Neville Chamberlain, from the cabinet room at 10 Downing Street, addressed the British nation. At dawn on the 1st Hitler's troops had swarmed across the Polish border in a full-scale invasion, and Poland was a country whose sovereignty had been guaranteed by Britain and France in an effort to deter German aggression. Germany had already occupied the Rhineland, a zone demilitarized by treaty between Germany and France. Hitler had absorbed Austria. He had received, without fighting, the Sudeten-German part of Czechoslovakia, largely at the instigation of Chamberlain, who had wished to appease him after hearing that this was Hitler's final demand in Europe. In the spring of 1939 Hitler had marched into Czechoslovakia itself. Poland was the next item on Hitler's menu. Chamberlain, with appeasement in tatters, had issued his guarantee. War became certain in August when the Soviets, who might have been concerned about Hitler's move to the east, to the consternation of Britain and France signed a pact with Hitler's Germany that gave the Nazis a free hand in Poland.

In a tired voice Chamberlain, who had striven for peace to the best of his ability — if perhaps not realistically — spoke into the microphone: "This morning the British ambassador in Berlin handed the German government a final note stating that unless the British government heard from them by 11 o'clock that they were prepared at once to withdraw their troops from Poland, a state of war would exist between us. I have to tell you now that no such assurance has been received, and that consequently this country is at war with Germany." The British people, after the tensions of the past few years caused by aggressive Nazi policies, accepted war with resignation and, in many cases, with

2. Neville Chamberlain

3. German troops march into Prague, the Czech capital.

3

relief. France, equally resigned to a second war with Germany within a generation, followed suit in declaring war, as did Canada on 10 September.

Chamberlain had made mistakes in the past, especially in his attempts to appease Hitler. His declaration of war was not one of them if Hitler was to be challenged before it was too late. Nor was his appointment of Winston Churchill as First Lord of the Admiralty the day before war was declared. Churchill, who had held the same job when the First World War had broken out and had prepared the Royal Navy for that war, understood the navy and had the strength of will and character to exercise decisive control. (Perhaps too much in the 1940 Norwegian campaign, when his personal dynamism led to wrong decisions.) The war would be fought on many fronts by land, on the sea and in the air, but the naval war was second to none in importance. Its main battleground was always the North Atlantic and, with war imminent, both sides stood ready in those waters.

4. Winston Churchill, First Lord of the Admiralty, arrives in France to discuss naval strategy with Admiral Darlan (right), Commander-in-Chief of the French navy.

German U-boats, in anticipation of the British move, were already patrolling the approaches to the British Isles. Two pocket battleships, *Graf Spee* and *Deutschland,* lurked in readiness far out in the Atlantic to begin the offensive. At 11 A.M. on the 3rd, when Britian's ultimatum had run out, the German navy's powerful transmitter radioed: "Battle stations immediately in accordance with instructions. . . ." Parallel actions, pushed vigorously by Churchill, were being undertaken by

British ships around the world and aimed at the blockade of Germany — seizing German shipping, stopping and searching neutral merchantmen bound for Germany, and bottling up Hitler's main fleet with mines and patrols.

On the evening of the 3rd, as dusk was gathering, the most westerly of the submarines (*U-30*) ringing the British Isles saw from the surface the 14,000-ton British passenger liner *Athenia*, which had that day rounded the northern tip of Ireland and was heading westwards into the open Atlantic on her way to Canada. The U-boat captain, 26-year-old Fritz Lemp — eager for action — ordered the boat to dive and attack. He stalked the defenceless vessel until he had the ship squarely in his periscope. In the torpedo compartment an engineer turned the cranks that gave the final settings to the torpedoes loaded in the tubes. When Lemp judged he was close enough to his target he gave the *Feuererlaubnis* (permission to fire), the trigger linked to the torpedo tubes was pulled to the shout "*Fächer eins — Los!*" (First salvo — Fire!) and two torpedoes, their motors running, streaked towards the liner with a "whoosh" of compressed air.

A shattering explosion holed the port side of the ship, wrecking the stairway to the upper deck and

5. SS *Athenia*.

trapping many passengers in a dining room and the decks below. The *Athenia* began to list and settle as the sea rushed in. Women and children were helped to the boats across the slanting deck.

Lemp surfaced with darkness to inspect his handiwork. After firing two shots at the mast to destroy the radio aerials and prevent the transmission of appeals for help, he left the scene. The radio worked, however, and destroyers and merchantmen sped to the rescue. It was not until the

Introduction

early hours that they arrived, to find *Athenia* still afloat surrounded by lifeboats. In all, 1,300 were rescued; 118 lost their lives, including some Canadians and a score of Americans, the first casualties of the Battle of the Atlantic that was to rage from this, the opening day, until hostilities ended in Europe. It was a war within the war, and Canada was in it from beginning to end.

How had it come about? For the origins of the Atlantic struggle we must go back to the First World War. The Second was in many ways merely a continuation of the First. Partners in some cases changed; technology had improved; but in the Atlantic we find the same opponents and roughly the same methods of waging war.

In the earlier war one main purpose of the Royal Navy was to keep Britain's sea lines of communication open; another was to sever those of the enemy, denying him the resources needed to continue waging war. Blockade is a weapon slow to take effect, but it exerted a powerful influence before the war was over.

Germany tried to break the stranglehold by reducing Britain's naval strength and command of the seas. The German High Seas Fleet was not powerful enough to challenge the Grand Fleet, if it remained concentrated, but it might be possible to fall upon its separate parts and destroy it piecemeal. That was the genesis of the Battle of Jutland, fought on 31 May 1916 in the North Sea off the coast of Denmark.

The German plan to bring only part of the Grand Fleet to action miscarried; instead it brought on the biggest battle in naval history, in which the British suffered the greater losses in ships and men. The British, however, were better able to afford the losses and the Grand Fleet continued to dominate the North Sea. The Germans risked no more major surface battles. The British blockade went on.

After Jutland Germany turned increasingly to submarine and mine warfare, the climax coming on 1 February 1917, when with about 140 submarines in commission she abandoned all restrictions and savagely attacked British, Allied and neutral ships alike — a campaign that soon (6 April) brought the United States into the war against her. The aim of the German U-boat (*Unterseeboot* or submarine) campaign was to sink so much shipping that not enough tonnage would remain to feed the British people (who relied on imports, then as now), maintain war industries and bring American troops and munitions across the Atlantic to confront the German armies in France. In the six months from the end of January 1917 to July Britain alone lost 2,350,000 tons of shipping; Allied and neutral nations lost 1,500,000. The position was extremely grave.

The staggering loss of 373 ships in April forced

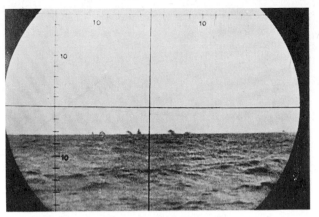
6. A convoy seen through a U-boat periscope.

7. The torpedo strikes.

8. Inferno.

Britain to consider the adoption of a convoy system whereby a group of merchant ships would cross the Atlantic under naval escort, an escort that would have the teeth to counteract the U-boat menace. Many opposed it. It was argued that the speed of the convoy would be reduced to the speed of the slowest ship; that the assemblage of shipping — 40 ships or so — would provide an irresistible target for torpedoes; and that merchant captains could not "keep station" in any case. Proponents maintained that the chief advantage would lie in the concentration of force (the escorts) around the object to be defended (the merchantmen) — a bit like a hunter tethering a goat and waiting for the tiger to come to him rather than searching the limitless jungle for the elusive quarry.

A partial convoy system was introduced in May 1917, and that month 287 ships were lost, 86 fewer than in April. A more comprehensive system came in during July, though it was not yet complete. Of all the 600 ships that sailed in convoy during July and August only three were torpedoed. It was clear that most of the ships still being sunk were either sailing independently, or had parted from their convoys.

By November 1917 — so convincing were the results — a complete convoy system was in full operation. Behind the ships at sea lay a worldwide organization for their control, assembly and marshalling into convoys according to destination and speed, and for the provision of escorts. In all the convoys formed in late 1917 the loss rate was no more than 1.25 per cent.

Karl Doenitz, a U-boat captain at the time and the man who was to command the German U-boat arm in the Second World War, pointed to the efficacy of the system:

The oceans at once became bare and empty; for long periods of time the U-boats, operating individually, would see nothing at all; and then, suddenly, up would loom a great convoy of ships, thirty or fifty or more of them, surrounded by an escort of warships of all types. The solitary U-boat . . . would then attack, thrusting again and again and persisting, if the commander had strong nerves, for several days and nights until the physical exhaustion of both commander and crew called a halt. The lone U-boat might well sink one or two of the ships, or even several, but that was but a poor percentage of the whole. The convoy would steam on. In most cases no other German U-boat would catch sight of it and it would reach Britain, bringing a rich cargo of foodstuffs and raw materials safely to port.

Still, the Germans knew how close they had come to starving Britain out of the war in 1917, and it is hardly surprising that a naval memorandum of October 1939 — after Poland had been crushed — pointed to the fact that Germany's "principal

9. U-boats at Kiel await orders to prowl the shipping lanes.

10. Target — convoy.

enemy," Britain, was vulnerable because of her maritime trade. The target, then, would be merchant ships, "not only the enemy's but every merchantman which sails the seas in order to supply the enemy's war interests. Military success can most confidently be expected if we attack British sea communications where they are most accessible to us with the greatest ruthlessness. The final aim of such attacks is to cut off all imports into and exports from Britain." Already, at the end of September, the two pocket battleships that had slipped out into distant Atlantic waters had received orders, as had submarines, to begin "the disruption and destruction" of enemy merchant shipping by all possible means. Nor was it surprising that with the outbreak of war the British had instigated a convoy system as far as the numbers of available escorts would permit.

After the First World War, fearing a resurgent Germany and remembering the fearful losses in merchant ships brought about by unrestricted U-boat warfare, Britain had pressed for the denial of *all* submarines to Germany. Under the Versailles Treaty they were strictly forbidden. Nevertheless long before Hitler — throughout the twenties — the navy secretly prepared to rebuild a U-boat arm and supported the work of a design and engineering team in Germany. Under cover of a firm registered in Holland, submarines were actually built for foreign powers, including Spain and Russia; and in these countries German crews and engineers participated in their trials. As early as 1928, on the basis of experience gained abroad, preparations began for the clandestine construction of 16 submarines in Germany itself.

That year Erich Raeder was appointed commander of the German navy at the age of 52. The son of a Hamburg teacher, he had fought at the Battle of Jutland. Cold, stern and reserved, he was a first-class strategist whose aim was to build a German fleet capable of holding its own against any other European power save Britain, a clash he wished to avoid. The Weimar Republic, concerned with economic matters, launched no new ships; despite violent Socialist opposition, however, Raeder piloted a proposal through the Reichstag

Introduction

11. The *Deutschland* undergoing inclining trials at Wilhemshaven. Over 10,000 tons and primarily armed with six 11-inch guns fore and aft, she fitted the limits imposed by the Treaty of Versailles. Neither a battleship nor exactly a cruiser, she was termed a "pocket battleship".

under which a new capital ship (some were permitted Germany under the Treaty of Versailles) would be completed soon after Hitler came to power. The 10,000 ton *Deutschland*, launched in April 1933, was a ship of revolutionary design. She mounted 11-inch guns that were more than a match for any cruiser, had a 21,500-mile cruising range and could outrun a battleship. With her power and speed she was aptly described as a "pocket battleship" and seemed to exemplify the current German naval thought that called for a fleet capable of breaking out of the North Sea to operate against shipping in the Atlantic — not, as in the earlier war, a battle fleet designed to challenge the Royal Navy's hold in the North Sea. Operations should be directed against the enemy's economic resources, not his armed forces. As one officer (Captain Waldemeyer Hartz) put it: "Attack upon the enemy's trade and protection for our own trade are the decisive tasks."

Though Raeder was not totally committed to this school of thought, his dream of a fleet of pocket

12. *Scharnhorst* had nine 11-inch guns in triple turrets. The Germans sacrificed weight of armament for speed and thicker protective plate. Catapult aircraft are astern.

battleships was influenced by it. The role of these ships, as wide-ranging raiders against enemy merchantmen, was carefully prepared. Germany, deprived of colonies, lacked overseas bases. Captain Wilhelm Franz Canaris (later Admiral Canaris, head of Military Counter-Intelligence — the *Abwehr*) revived a First War secret supply organization in ports all over the world whose agents would report on the disposition of merchant vessels and arrange for German ships to receive supplies.

In Hitler, who came to power in 1933, Raeder soon found a man who would support his dream. But it was two years before Hitler felt strong enough to throw off the shackles of Versailles. In March 1935 he renounced the treaty and the limitations it imposed on Germany, announcing the setting up of the *Luftwaffe*, the introduction of conscription and the building of two battleships. Germany was on the march. The prefabricated parts of a number of U-boats were ordered to be assembled, though this Hitler did not announce as yet.

The new battleships, *Scharnhorst* and *Gneisenau* (classed by the British as battle-cruisers) would not, it was said, exceed 25,000 tons. Thus the Washington Naval Treaty limits established to prevent a naval arms race between Britain, the United States and Japan would not be contravened. Their true displacement when built, however, was 35,000 tons. Germany had been excluded from the negotiations that had led to the Washington Treaty (which, amongst other things, had limited the size of the navies of Britain, the United States and Japan in accordance with a 5:5:3 ratio, France and Italy both settling for 1.75) and there was no knowing how far Hitler would go. Britain, anxious to contain any threat, was willing to make concessions towards a limited German navy.

Germany offered, during discussions held in London that summer, not to exceed 35 per cent of British strength. The Admiralty counselled acceptance "before the demand should be increased." And, as it was obvious that Hitler would build submarines anyway, the British were

13. *Gneisenau*.

happy to accept a self-imposed German limitation — 45 per cent of the British tonnage — though it was conceded that the Germans might have full parity "on due notification." The Anglo—German Naval Agreement was signed on 18 June 1935. Eleven days later the Germans launched *U-1*, the first of their new U-boats. Such rapid implementation must have given the British food for thought.

14. Grand Admiral Erich Raeder at a pre-war naval review.

15. Karl Doenitz (when Grand Admiral).

In September of that year Raeder summoned Captain Karl Doenitz, then captain of the old cruiser *Emden*, to take command of the first flotilla of nine new U-boats at Kiel. By 1939 Doenitz had six flotillas. Of the 57 U-boats, 38 were of the early type (Type II), 250 tons, strong and manoeuvrable, but of short range; these were modified in 1940 to permit Altantic use. The remaining 19 were larger Type VII oceangoing boats, a type that was to be the backbone of the U-boat fleet throughout the war. A successful U-boat captain in the First World War, Doenitz was the right man to command the U-boat arm. Short, slim, jug-eared and with a drooping mouth, Doenitz was not impressive, but underneath this outward appearance lay two great qualities. The first was a concern for the welfare of his crews and his knack of greeting and talking with every man; at sea he would drive them to a point just short of their limits. He would do his best *for* them, and he expected the best *from* them; he got it. His second was his undoubted ability, based on his personal knowledge of what a U-boat could do and his keeping abreast of tactical and technological developments. Doenitz's men were treated as elite, and sensed that they were; their morale was high. He lost no time in forging the U-boat arm into a highly effective weapon.

War against Britain and France, which they had been told to plan for in 1944, came far too quickly

16. *U-1*, and a later (Type II) pre-war U-boat. Both were prefabricated and assembled in record time.

Introduction

17. *U-52*, a pre-war (Type VIIB) U-boat. The Type VIIC boat, which was similar, was the most widely used German submarine of the Second World War.

to suit either Raeder or Doenitz. The latter had told his chief (who pressed it on Hitler) that he required 300 U-boats to ensure a decisive result against British commerce; in September 1939 he had 57. Raeder had been ordered in November 1937 — against his own inclinations — to plan a fleet powerful enough to challenge the Royal Navy. His plans for pocket battleships and U-boats, which could be quickly implemented for mercantile warfare, had to be altered to include battleships and aircraft carriers that would give a balanced force

capable of standing up to the Royal Navy. All this, he estimated, could not be completed before 1948, but he did not oppose Hitler. He adopted the so-called Z Plan, which, with Hitler's decision to crush Poland in 1939, forced him into a hopeless race against time. The Z-Plan Fleet, as originally conceived and modified, was to have consisted of four parts: a fleet, strong enough to meet the British Home Fleet, of four battleships, two heavy cruisers and flotillas of destroyers; a raiding force for use against British commerce of three pocket battleships, five cruisers, five light cruisers and 247

18. Hitler, with Raeder (right foreground), at a naval review.

U-boats by 1948; and two *attack* forces, each of one aircraft carrier, three battleships, two cruisers and enough destroyers for protection.

When Britain and France declared war because of Hitler's invasion of Poland, all Raeder had was three pocket battleships (*Deutschland, Admiral Graf Spee* and *Admiral Scheer*), two new battle cruisers that were virtually battleships (*Scharnhorst* and *Gneisenau),* a new heavy cruiser, five light cruisers, 17 destroyers and 57 submarines. Two monster battleships (*Bismarck* and *Tirpitz*) and two cruisers (*Blücher* and *Prinz Eugen*) were completing and two aircraft carriers were planned, one of which (*Graf Zeppelin*) was launched in December 1938 but did not see service.

The British outnumbered the Reich 7:1 in battleships, 6:1 in cruisers, 9:1 in destroyers. Only two German carriers were being built against Britain's six. The U-boat arm had only one-sixth of the strength that Doenitz wanted. The "power of audacity", then, had to take the place of a fleet that was approved but which was not yet in being.

Despite this, Germany's naval problems were much simpler than those of Great Britain. The relative weakness in surface ships automatically ruled out "sea battle" confrontations with the Royal Navy. Nor could a British blockade be prevented; it was recognized, with cold realism, that when war came there would be no German overseas commerce through the North Sea and across the Atlantic Ocean.

Two main tasks remained and both, it was hoped, could be realized. The first was to retain control of the Baltic Sea and thus protect the sea lanes from Norway and Sweden by means of which ore from Swedish mines — vital to German war production — came in either directly across the Baltic or via Norway's coastal waters. Germany's surface fleet, incomplete though it was, could outmatch any possible combination of Baltic nations and was strong enough to bar the narrow straits between Denmark and Sweden against any British incursions, especially when supported by German aircraft.

Secondly — a nightmare to the Admiralty — the Germans determined to attack British merchant shipping and British ports by means of mines, aircraft, submarines and surface ships in order to cut off food and raw materials and so starve Britain out of the war. U-boats had improved since 1917. Wide-ranging pocket battleships would be too powerful for the small naval ships that the British were expected to use for the protection of convoys. The British would not be able to afford such depredations: they would be forced to use large warships for escort duty, thus dissipating their strength.

The Admiralty, as in the First World War, planned the establishment of a naval blockade that would cut off all of Germany's seaborne trade. Germany did not depend so much on overseas commerce as did Britain; and thanks to her ally Italy and the Nazi-Soviet pact of August 1939, which guaranteed the delivery of Russian supplies, Germany was less vulnerable than she had been in the earlier war. Yet the delivery of supplies by rail, with German railroads congested not only by normal traffic but by military traffic as well, would be a difficult and expensive business. Though only partially effective when imposed in September 1939, and less so when the Nazis overran western Europe in 1940 and pillaged the countries they occupied, blockade grew in importance from mid-1941 (when the Nazis invaded Russia and lost Soviet deliveries) and was a major factor in victory after 1944 when the occupied countries were being freed and German economic resources were drying up.

19. Launching mines from a British minelayer. A mine barrage was one of the methods employed to blockade German ports.

20. Naval and Customs officers inspect cargo in the hold of a neutral vessel bound for Germany — part of the British blockade of Hitler's Reich.

Introduction

The Royal Navy, as always, would support ground operations as called for. This it was to do in Norway and France (1940), during the Allied invasions of North Africa, Sicily and Italy, and — massively — on D-Day, 1944. Overseas contingents, from Australia, Canada, India and New Zealand as well as troop convoys from the United States, were always heavily protected. Provision for the convoy bringing the 1st Canadian Division to England in 1939, for example, had consisted of HMS *Resolution* (battleship), close escort; two British and four Canadian destroyers, local escort; HMS *Furious* (aircraft carrier), HMS *Repulse* (battle cruiser) and HMS *Emerald* (cruiser), acting as a covering force.

The protection of the sea lanes supplying Britain was a task that continued throughout the war. The British Isles, heavily industrialized, produced only half the food consumed by their 50 million inhabitants and the other half came in by ships. And the industries — ever since Munich turning out guns, tanks, aircraft and ships at full pitch — required raw materials that had to come by sea, for Britain had few resources. Over the vast spaces of the oceans of the world merchant ships carried valuable cargoes to or from Britain, and somehow they had to be protected. Britain had nowhere near as many cruisers and destroyers as she had possessed in the First World War, and she was aware that German submarines were more effective. Though the convoy system came into force with war, escorts could be spared only for use in the dangerous waters of the eastern North Atlantic where the shipping lanes converged — the "Western Approaches" to the British Isles.

The adoption of the convoy system, as was necessary, was in itself a victory for the Germans. It slowed the shipment of badly-needed supplies. Ships were forced to wait while a convoy assembled; the speed of faster ships had to be reduced to that of the slowest, for though convoys were classed as "slow" (less than ten knots) and "fast" (10–15 knots), there were still differences in the speeds of ships so that a slow convoy would average about seven knots and a fast one only about ten. The route taken was not necessarily the most direct for all the ships; finally, the arrival of a convoy at the destination, all the ships requiring unloading, resulted in congestion and further delay. All this cut the effective cargo-carrying capacity of ships by one-third, a not insignificant factor in the "tonnage war."

That Canada would in time provide half the protection for the vital North Atlantic route could not have been foreseen. Mackenzie King had turned away from any "collective security" arrangement in advance of war, but when war came between Britain and Germany, Parliament decided, by an

21. Encouragment in crisis.

overwhelming majority, to join the struggle. Canada had virtually no navy to send anywhere — a mere six destroyers and a handful of minesweepers. Even that was fortunate; in the grim days of the Depression the fate of the Royal Canadian Navy had been seriously in doubt. Canada, from the first, assumed a share in the Battle of the Atlantic and set out to build up a large front-line navy, mostly from her own shipyards. By the end of the war Canada had a navy of almost a 100,000 personnel and 400 ships, as we shall see; a fact that, in the long, close struggle that lay ahead, was decisive.

Britain had also to bear in mind the possibility of an outbreak of fighting in the Mediterranean (termed by Italy "Mare Nostrum" — our sea), where Mussolini, Hitler's partner, seemed bent on war. And there had to be some naval strength in the Far East, where Japan, Hitler's other partner, was becoming more aggressive day by day. Naval resources were limited, however, and those sent to the Far East were to prove inadequate.

The Mediterranean was vital to the successful waging of a European war. Oil from Persia and Burma, and rubber from Malaya travelled through it, via the Suez Canal. Iraqi oil, pumped across the desert, reached the Eastern Mediterranean at Haifa and at Tripoli. The Mediterranean route was the one that Britain would use to send troops and military supplies to defend her interests in the Mediterranean (Gibraltar, Malta, Cyprus), Egypt and East Africa, and the Far East. Along this route would come the contingents from Australia, India and New Zealand to bolster the outnumbered British armies. Britain could count on French help, and the French fleet was strong enough to contain the Italian. After France fell in 1940, however, there had to be a strong naval force in the Mediterranean; but that meant fewer ships to safeguard the North Atlantic convoys.

Both Germany and Britain stuck to their basic plans throughout the war, though these were modified with war's changing fortunes. When Germany invaded Russia, for example, the British assumed an extra commitment — to send supplies to Russia, which meant furnishing extra naval ships. The merchantmen crossing the North Atlantic were a vital concern to the belligerents throughout the war.

Since Britain lost most of her merchant ships in the North Atlantic, it is of interest to know the state of her mercantile fleet at the outbreak of the war. It was the largest in the world (3,000 ships), close to the combined total of its next three rivals, the United States (1,409), Japan (1,054) and Norway (816). But the Depression had hit Britain hard; ships had been laid up and there had been little new construction. The ships on which Britain was to depend for survival in 1939 were largely aging and dilapidated. Canada could not help much. She had maintained a merchant fleet — even a government-operated one — between the wars. Faced with serious Allied shipping losses in the First World War, Canada had decided early in 1918 to build and operate merchant ships. In all, 66 were built, but too late, as it turned out, for the war. Operated successfully as the Canadian Government Merchant Marine in the boom years immediately following peace, they began to lose money in the recession of 1921. The smaller and less profitable vessels were disposed of, and in 1936, as a result of the Depression, the government got rid of the remaining ships. Financially the venture had been disastrous; but it had created a large number of experienced masters and seamen that the Allies would be glad of in 1939.

In the British merchant service the officers were usually men of good education who had gone to sea following a family tradition. Their pay was low. The seamen, engine-room men and catering staff, abysmally paid, were usually natives of London, Liverpool, Cardiff, Glasgow, Hull or Southampton — north-country men, southerners, Scots and Welsh. In cramped ships — average about 7,000 tons — they ate unappetizing food (a minimum scale of fresh food was stipulated in the Merchant

22. Alexandria, Egypt — Britain's main naval base in the eastern Mediterranean.

23. Freighters such as these were Britain's mainstay during the early years of the Battle of the Atlantic. Top, SS *Clarissa Radcliffe*, 6,000 tons, built 1915, foundered in a storm 7 March 1943, when carrying iron ore. Centre, SS *Nariva*, 9,000 tons, built 1920, sunk by a U-boat on the night 15/16 March 1943. Bottom, SS *Coacero*, 7,000 tons, built 1923, sunk by a U-boat 17 March 1943.

Introduction

Shipping Act, but the substitution of salt or canned meat was permitted ''with reasonable cause,'' and the causes were invariably stated to be ''reasonable''). They endured crossings that averaged a fortnight in peacetime in cramped and uncomfortable quarters and in all sorts of weather. Weather was always a hazard on North Atlantic crossings. Fogs, gales, enormous seas and ice — which in certain conditions encrusted a ship's superstructure so thickly that the vessel would founder or capsize — had always to be reckoned with.

The coming of the war made very little difference to the composition of the crews of merchantmen. It made employment (somewhat whimsical in the years of economic depression) more certain. Many ships, laid up in the Depression (and others fit only for the scrapyard) were brought back into service and required crews. Young men joined the service

24. SS *Aldermin* (top) a Dutch freighter of 8,000 tons, built in 1920. SS *Granville* (centre) Norwegian freighter of 4-5,000 tons, built 1930. SS *Port Auckland* (bottom) British, 9,000 tons, built shortly before the war. All these ships were sunk by U-boats in early 1943.

— those who preferred to join the merchant navy rather than the armed forces. Discipline was less rigorous, pay (though low) was higher and a man had a chance to see the world. A merchant sailor could exercise a certain amount of choice: after one voyage he was offered another ship, which he could refuse; also a second. But if he refused a third he was immediately called up for military service. As a result he was not usually condemned to one North Atlantic crossing, with all its suspense, after another; a long voyage through fairly safe, and at least warm, waters to Australia or New Zealand might intervene (as might the Arctic run to Russia, which was really hated). Most men liked the gamble — it could be the *Queen Mary* on one voyage and a tramp steamer the next. These men bore the brunt of the Atlantic war. Classed as a civilian occupation, one-quarter of the men of the merchant navy died during the war years, a higher percentage of total casualties than those suffered by either the army, navy or air force — the fighting services.

At the outbreak of the war Canada had only 38 oceangoing merchant ships of 1,000 tons or more, totalling less than 250,000 tons. U-boats, in their best-performance months, sank more tonnage than that in a fortnight. She was to build 456 merchant ships (with a deadweight capacity just short of four million tons), but before shipbuilding got started Canadian merchant seamen went to sea in whatever vessels could be rounded up, mostly Great Lakes steamers and coasters that were never intended for the open sea, as well as in larger freighters, Canadian and British, and passenger ships. The great Canadian Pacific liners — *The Empress of Britain, The Empress of Australia* and others — though under British registry were Canadian, as were the ''Duchess'' ships. The writer, when a young army officer in 1940, sailed round the Cape to Egypt in the *Duchess of York*.

For low pay (a wage of $75–$100 a month plus a war risk of $44.50) and often bad food (though it was better than British), they faced the hazards of weather and U-boats, the prospects of death in icy water or blazing oil, and still signed on for more. Unlike naval crews, they wore no uniforms, got little recognition for what they did, and had few amenities in the ports. Yet in fair weather, in fog or storms, they took the ships — herded into crowded columns, showing no lights, and observing radio silence so that the danger of collision was always present — time after time from one side of the Atlantic to the other. Convoys were led by a commodore — often a retired British admiral who had left his peaceful home to do his bit — to control the ships, to liaise with escort leaders and to establish the rules that would be followed by the merchant captains throughout the voyages. At

25. Convoy conference at Halifax. Merchant captains and naval officers study orders and are briefed before sailing.

26. A merchant captain peers into the fog that greatly increased the possibility of collision while in convoy.

those of faster ships in slow convoys, deliberately "romped" or "ran" — steaming out of the convoy lines to take their chances alone. Peacetime practices were scrapped in the interests of concealment from the U-boats: furnaces had to be stoked carefully to guard against making giveaway smoke; bilges could not be pumped for fear of leaving slicks of oil; garbage had to be retained for disposal at the ports. But merchant seamen counted themselves lucky, despite the conditions of their service, when the wet, stinking, uncomfortable ships got through.

sea the difficult task of controlling the merchantmen fell to the commodore, who kept his navy-trained signaller busy warning straying vessels to keep position — a matter that called for many adjustments of revolutions to hold a constant speed. Station-keeping was chaotic with the first convoys, but it improved with practice. Zigzagging called for more complicated procedures that caused mounting tension in the early days. The commodore had to be tactful in using his authority when dealing with independent-minded masters, but the captains of naval escorts were not always so; grizzled merchant skippers felt they had forgotten more about seamanship than young naval officers would ever know and tempers flared. Some captains, especially

27. Stoker.

Introduction

28. Atlantic convoy under attack.

Many did not. Sixty-eight Canadian merchant ships were lost in the course of the war, and in fact the last ship to be sunk by the U-boats, the *Avondale Park*, was Canadian. More than a thousand Canadian seamen (1,148) lost their lives throughout the war. The war memorial at Halifax lists the names of 1,059 who have no known graves, other than the sea; the almost 100 others died from exposure, wounds, sickness or other causes after the ships had reached port. Their graves are known.

Veterans whose vessels were sunk — often more than once — describe the anxiety of the voyages; the feeling of vulnerability when no more than the thickness of the hull separated them from the angry seas; and the knowledge that a torpedo, streaking towards the ship, could shatter in an instant the protection afforded by the steel plates. And the terror, when the worst had happened with the

sudden burst and smell of high explosive, of leaping from the unnaturally slanting decks into the angry foam below; the shock of hitting water and the desperate struggle to keep from being sucked towards the still-racing propellers or into the vortex that the sinking ship would leave. They remember the cries of others, struggling in the water, fighting for life as they were themselves. Some spent days in open boats, using the oars to keep from being swamped, soaked to the skin, with men dying as the days wore on. Those who died were gently lowered over the side, said one survivor, "with care and reverence." The Canadian destroyer *Skeena*, directed to the distress signal from a lifeboat in September 1942, could not find it in the vast expanse despite the intermittent transmissions that she received. Then nothing was heard. She searched but found no more than the empty sea.

The efforts of these men were the basis on which the final outcome of the war in Europe depended;

29. The fortunate were rescued.

30. Boat from HMCS *Sarnia* (minesweeper) picks up survivors off Halifax.

and that is why, in this account of Canada's part in the Battle of the Atlantic, they have been mentioned first. They transported the food and raw materials on which Britain's survival rested; and they brought the weapons, even the vast armies, that made

Britain the stepping-stone to the liberation of western Europe. Without them the war might well have had a different ending. They could not have done this, however, without naval, and later air, support.

The role of the Royal Canadian Navy has been denigrated by some recent, revisionist historians, but it should not be. Rising from small beginnings (six destroyers, five minesweepers and a naval strength, including reserves, of about 3,000 in 1939), Canada was to operate during the war 471 ships manned or administered by very close to 90,000 officers and men; 6,500 women enlisted in the Women's Royal Canadian Naval Services — freeing men to go to sea. Almost two thousand (1,990) members of the RCN gave up their lives. That alone, expressed in terms of dry statistics, is no mean record.

Through the war years Canada produced almost 400 naval ships herself. These included four destroyers, 122 corvettes, 70 frigates (improved, twin-screw corvettes), and 122 minesweepers that were especially useful in clearing the invasion routes on D-Day, 1944. She manned escort carriers in the North Atlantic and other British ships. Of all these ships, 24 were lost, some of which will be noted. They accounted for 29 U-boats, 17 of them after 1943 when training, experience and cohesion

31. Secrecy, with regard to troop or ship movements, had to be maintained, as this Canadian poster attests.

Introduction

32. *Blücher*, sunk by the Norwegians in Oslo Fjord.

had made the RCN a really effective force. Navies cannot be created overnight. It takes time to build ships and train their crews. And without a sufficient fleet in being when war breaks out, that long process must be accepted. Canadians served their apprenticeship, they learned the lessons; by the spring of 1943 they were shouldering half the North Atlantic burden. In mid-1944, so thoroughly had the fight against U-boats been won, Canadian escorts shepherded a massive convoy of 167 merchant ships, carrying a million tons of cargo to Britain, without the loss of a single ship.

The war was fought roughly as envisaged by both sides for the remaining months of 1939 and until April 1940. In that time the Allies lost merchant ships, even warships, but the losses were not insupportable; the Germans lost U-boats and one pocket battleship, so that the score was roughly even in terms of relative strengths.

On 9 April 1940 however, the Germans seized Denmark and invaded Norway; already, at the end of March, U-boats had been sent to Norway ready to help in that campaign. The Norwegians fought for two months and remained at war until June; King Haakon and his government were brought to London by sea just before the end. They scored some successes, notably by sinking the German cruiser *Blücher*, carrying troops, in Oslo fjord. The British, who came to the aid of the Norwegians, lost ships (one aircraft carrier and five destroyers) but the Germans lost far more (three cruisers and 10

33. Chamberlain bows out.

Introduction

destroyers); moreover three heavier ships, all damaged, remained out of commission during the summer, a time when Hitler needed every ship for his projected invasion of Britain. The navy that remained was far too weak to be of much use.

Germany, however, gained territory of strategic importance — sheltered Norwegian harbours for surface ships and U-boat bases flanking the North Atlantic. Aircraft from fields in the north of Norway were to take a heavy toll when convoys carried aid to Russia later in the war.

British troops, who had had little success, were withdrawn from Norway. All that the British saw was humiliation and defeat. Chamberlain, who was blamed, was forced to resign as the result of a debate on the campaign in the House of Commons. Churchill, who as First Lord of the Admiralty was largely responsible for the campaign — and the fiasco — became Prime Prime Minister on 10 May.

On that day, early in the morning and with no declaration of war, Hitler unleashed his *Wehrmacht* against the Netherlands, Luxembourg and Belgium. A cloud of parachutists seized airfields and bridges in the Netherlands ahead of the main columns, and the neutral Dutch, with weak forces, were overwhelmed. Queen Wilhelmina, the government and the small navy crossed to Britain on the 13th. Two days later, after Rotterdam had been levelled from the air, all resistance ceased. Meanwhile tiny Luxembourg had fallen without resistance, and by the evening of 11 May the Belgians, having lost the Meuse bridges, were falling back.

It was then the turn of France. Believing that the rugged Ardennes country was impossible for armour, the French had neglected to defend it properly. It was across this terrain that the Germans struck. On 13 May the Germans were over the French border. They crossed the Meuse at several points, including Sedan, where, bombed by screaming Stuka divebombers, the French panicked and fled. On that day France lost the war. By the 20th German armour had reached the Channel coast. A panzer wedge had been driven between the northern force (a million French, Belgians and British) and the main French forces to the south. On 20 May King Leopold of the Belgians made it clear that his troops were no longer capable of offensive

35. Modern heavy cruisers of the Italian navy moored in Naples harbour. All three were destroyed by the Royal Navy off Cape Matapan on the night 28/29 March, 1941.

action. The evacuation of British troops from Dunkirk began on the night 26–27 May. On 22 June the French made peace with Germany, signing a humiliating document which placed all northern (industrial) France under German occupation, as well as the entire Atlantic coast, including Biscay, as far as the Spanish frontier. The rest of France south of the Loire — and here Hitler, anxious to prevent the French fleet and colonial empire from going over to the British, showed moderation — would remain nominally French under a government, headed by 84-year-old Marshal Pétain, soon to be installed at Vichy.

The Italian dictator, Mussolini — Hitler's Axis partner — declared war on 10 June when the defeat of France was certain and it was obviously safe to do so. With that he added the Italian navy, roughly as strong as the French,* to that of Germany. Thus Britain, deprived of French help, found the Italian fleet pitted against her; she would have to safeguard her interests in the Mediterranean alone.

The French fleet, the armistice terms stated, would be disarmed and remain in French ports. It would not be seized, Hitler promised, by Germany.

*	Battleships	Aircraft Carriers	Heavy Cruisers	Light Cruisers	Destroyers	Submarines
FRANCE	9 (+3 under construction)	1 (+2)	7 (+1)	12 (+3)	78 (+27)	75 (+38)
ITALY	6 (+2)	—	7	15 (+12)	59 (+5)	112 (+17)

34. British troops, evacuated from Dunkirk, crowd the deck of a destroyer.

36. The French fleet at Mers-el-Kebir under attack, 3 July, 1940.

But Britain could not rely on that. Without the French fleet, and with full responsibility for the Mediterranean, Britain — now that invasion threatened — was in great danger. If the ships fell into German hands she could quickly lose the war. Churchill acted. The French warships in British ports, which had been recalled to France, were seized on the night of 3 July.

At Mers-el-Kebir (in Algeria, near Oran) the Royal Navy opened fire after an ultimatum to the effect that the French warships there must sail for British ports or scuttle themselves had been refused; two battleships and one battle-cruiser were sunk, causing the loss of more than a thousand French sailors' lives. Another warship, at Dakar, was crippled by torpedo bombers on 8 July. A battleship and four cruisers at Alexandria agreed to demilitarize themselves. Thus a large number of ships were prevented from joining the remainder of the fleet at Toulon, and the Royal Navy retained its superiority. In retaliation Pétain broke off diplomatic relation with Britain. This was of not much importance. The "Vichy" French collaborated fully with the Germans from the start; and both Pétain and his foreign minister, Pierre Laval, expected — and desired — the defeat of Britain. France furnished enough oil for Germany to fight the Battle of Britain and the initial campaign in Russia; she was to provide a division (the Charlemagne) to fight with Hitler's legions. There is little doubt that, in these first days of occupation and what Pétain called "the French State" (with himself as Chief), collaboration with victorious Germany was popular in France. Most people prefer to be on the winning side.

As it was, Hitler had conquered France both

cheaply and with incredible speed. Even tiny Norway had held out longer than the much-vaunted French, whose army had generally been considered the best in Europe. Britain had been weakened, not merely by the loss of the weapons and equipment of the British Expeditionary Force; she had lost six destroyers in the Battle of France and nearly 200 fighter aircraft she could ill afford. There had been no real bleeding of the German army — and Hitler had gained French resources to make him far stronger than before. Mussolini had finally entered the war to make the Berlin–Rome Axis a reality, ranging Italy's army, navy and air force on Hitler's side.

Only the British Commonwealth and some national contingents from the occupied countries remained at war with the Axis. The USA was still predominantly isolationist, and the USSR was positively engaged on the Axis side. If one considers Britain's predicament, the widespread belief that the Nazis had won will not seem absurd. A great many more people held that view than were prepared to admit it three or four years later.

With the loss of so much of Europe, imports, which had come economically from the Continent, had to come from far afield. This increased the length of voyages and meant the delivery of fewer cargoes. From midsummer the Germans had U-boat bases in the French Biscay Ports of Lorient, Brest, La Pallice, St. Nazaire and Bordeaux, which, since the Straits of Dover were effectively closed by a British minefield, were reached by way of Norway and the passage between the Faeröes and Iceland. In France the Germans had many advantages. U-boats, closer to the scene of operations, could extend their range by 450 miles and strike farther into the ocean. When facilities for the servicing of

37 A U-boat leaves its new base at St. Nazaire.

boats were installed, boats could be sent back to sea without returning to Germany; this added 10 days to the time a U-boat could spend in its operational area — the equivalent, it has been estimated, of an increase in U-boat strength of 40 per cent. The Germans also had air bases across the Channel from England, and from these they made the southern ports of England completely untenable. British coastal ships bound from west- to east-coast ports could no longer use the Channel; they had to sail round the north of Scotland, a voyage that took 11 days, there and back.

Moreover, a large percentage of Britain's naval resources was held to counter German invasion, a threat that loomed throughout the summer. This was done, as it had to be, at the expense of escorting the North Atlantic convoys.

When Italy entered the war, the Mediterranean was closed to merchant ships. Shipping followed the Cape route around Africa instead. That meant voyages of 13,000 miles to Suez, instead of 3,000; and of nearly 11,000 to Bombay, instead of 6,000.

But not everything was on the debit side. Poland, when invaded, had put three destroyers and 13 merchantmen at Britain's disposal. Though Denmark continued to be neutral despite German occupation (King Christian and his government remained in Copenhagen), 90 per cent of Danish ships outside German ports (about 43) and 5,000 seamen eventually joined the Allies. In June 1940 a mere 5 per cent of French ships outside France responded to the appeal of General de Gaulle, the "Free French" leader, but foreign ships, chartered to France, transferred their charters to the British. Other ships came from the Netherlands (a small naval fleet and 147 merchantmen) and Belgium (again, a navy of small ships and 34 freighters). The

38. Three of Poland's four destroyers leave Gdynia to join the Royal Navy. The destroyer that remained (foreground) was lost during the defence of Gdynia.

39. A Danish freighter, which joined the Allies, offloads supplies.

40. Dutch minesweepers on the way to Britain.

41. A Norwegian merchant seaman — one of 30,000 who joined the Allied cause.

42. Russian women at Murmansk load a cargo of arms, delivered from Britain, for the front.

greatest acquisition of all came from Norway, whose merchant fleet was the fourth largest in the world. A thousand ships (4 million gross tons) manned by 30,000 seamen eventually augmented the British merchant fleet, a large proportion of them tankers. These were to carry about 40 per cent of the oil required in the different theatres of war. And Sweden, though neutral, promised Britain 60 per cent of her dry-cargo tonnage outside the Baltic (480,000 deadweight tons), a pledge she was to fulfil. More ships were to come following the German invasions of Yugoslavia and Greece in 1941, so that future Atlantic convoys — though under British control, for the British hired the ships and paid the crews — were, in composition, something of a United Nations in embryo. Within these families of seagoing ships, like any other family, there were disputes. Language problems sometimes complicated control. Harsh words were spoken from time to time. But the masters of these ships were never asked to take a larger share than might in justice be asked of them, and differences, which were not serious, tended to melt in the face of common danger.

This augmentation did not take place overnight. Ships of these nations had been scattered all over the world when their homelands were seized by Germany, and they were drawn into service over many months. Despite them — and their contribution to the winning of the Battle of the Atlantic was considerable — Britain's maritime position after the fall of France was far less strong than it had been at the outbreak of war.

1939-1940 Britain's vulnerability increases

Britain, at the start of the war, imported 55 million tons of food and raw materials every year, the bulk of it through Atlantic waters. The shipping routes from Australia, India and Africa (round the Cape), as well as those from South America and the eastern seaboard of the United States and Canada, all converged in the Western Approaches to the British Isles. This, therefore, was the principal danger area. Britain depended heavily on Canadian wheat and lumber; and on U.S. phosphates (and other minerals), cotton, and manufactured products such as machine tools. Of all the sea routes supplying Britain, the one across the North Atlantic from American and Canadian ports carried much the greatest weight of traffic.

Britain was far from being self-sufficient. Were her vital imports to be cut off or seriously curtailed, she could not survive even in peacetime. In time of war she required even greater imports, especially of arms, to oppose the military and industrial power of Germany. The Germans, aware that seaborne commerce was essential to Britain's survival, determined from the start to cut the sea routes with all the means at their disposal: capital ships and armed merchant raiders to sink merchantmen on the high seas; mines and aircraft to blast ships in coastal waters; and, above all, U-boats — which were the most effective. It will be seen that the resulting Battle of the Atlantic, fought by capital ships on both sides, by aircraft and through rival technologies, as well as by submarines and convoy escorts, was perhaps the most crucial, as well as the fiercest confrontation of the war. It was waged from the first day of European hostilities to the last, and Canada was in it from the start.

At the outset Hitler had ordered U-boats to observe the rules of the Hague Convention, whereby a submarine must first stop its intended victim, then order its crew to take to the boats, and only after that had been done — sink the ship; this, however, did not apply to ships in convoy. The sinking of the unescorted passenger liner *Athenia* without warning — only hours after Neville Chamberlain's announcement of a state of war — was a direct contravention by the U-boat commander of the order, which Hitler had issued because he hoped to come to terms with Britain and France after the defeat of Poland; he had therefore not wished to antagonize those countries unduly. The German navy, however, wanted no restrictions. A merchant ship might use its radio while the warning was being given, thus putting the U-boat in danger; and the responsibility for picking up any survivors for whom there were no boats would reduce the U-boat's ability to continue operations. Within three months, with Poland defeated and Britain and France still at war, Hitler dropped all restrictions; from that time on little mercy was ever shown to merchant sailors. They, in turn, and their escorts, adopted a policy of "sink on sight"; they hunted U-boats to their death. The crews of U-boats, which invariably dived when detected, stood little chance in a crippled "iron coffin." There were few survivors.

Both sides were handicapped during the first two years of the struggle. The Germans had insufficient submarines; the Allies insufficient escorts or technology. Basically, the Germans lacked U-boats in sufficient numbers to bring decisive results. They used mines (including the unconventional magnetic mine which was triggered by the metal bulk of a ship passing over it), surface warships, armed

43. Canadian newspapers pointed to Canadian passengers aboard *Athenia* at a time when Canada was not, officially, yet at war.

THE WEATHER
Cloudy—Warm

The Ottawa Morning Journal

TEMPERATURE
Minimum—60
Maximum—79

NO. 21237.　　　　　　　OTTAWA, MONDAY, SEPTEMBER 4, 1939.　　　　　　　PRICE THREE CENTS

BRITISH LINER ATHENIA WITH 1,400 ABOARD TORPEDOED AND SUNK WEST OF SCOTLAND

Canadians and Americans Majority of Passengers On Stricken Steamship

Liner Was Bound for Montreal With Refugees—Roosevelt Receives News With Horror—McAdoo Says Outrage May Force U.S. Into War

LONDON, Sept. 4.—(C.P.)—The British liner Athenia with 1,400 passengers aboard, most of them Canadians and Americans, was torpedoed and sunk today.

The Ministry of Information announced that the 13,581-ton ship reported to the admiralty she had been torpedoed 200 miles off the Hebrides, west of northern Scotland.

She was bound from Liverpool for Montreal.

The Ministry of information said the last official information received by the admiralty from the ship was that she was sinking "rapidly". Since there were no further advices, it was assumed she had gone down.

There was no hint as to injuries or rescues of passengers.

LINER ATHENIA

It was said, however, the Athenia was adequately equipped with lifeboats.

Well-known in the Glasgow Montreal trade, the Athenia is owned by the Donaldson Atlantic Line, Ltd., a firm associated with the Cunard White Star Line.

The Athenia is 526 feet long and was built in 1923 at Glasgow. She has a breadth of 66 feet and a depth of 38 feet. The Athenia recently reconditioned on an extensive scale involving reconstruction of her entire passenger quarters.

Reported to Roosevelt.

WASHINGTON, Sept. 3.—(P)—Stephen Early, secretary to President Roosevelt, said tonight that the torpedoed Athenia was "carrying mostly Canadians and some Americans," according to official reports received here.

Mr. Roosevelt received an official despatch telling of the torpedoing.

The reports said the ship was "rapidly sinking."

"I'd like to point out", Early said, "that according to official information the ship had come from Glasgow to Liverpool and was bound for Canada bringing refugees.

"I point this out to show that there was no possibility, according to the official information, that the ship was carrying any munitions, or anything of that kind."

Report Received With Horror.

The report was received with obvious horror at the White House. When reporters, seeking more information after Early had made his announcement asked "Is that all?" Early replied: "Isn't that enough?"

Ambassador Kennedy sent the following message from London:

"Report steamship Athenia, of Donaldson Line, torpedoed 200 miles off Maylin Head, with 1,400 passengers aboard. SOS received. Ship sinking fast."

Ambassador Kennedy reported later that the British Admiralty had so far been unable to determine whether the Athenia had sunk or whether rescue arrangements were being made.

246 Americans Lose Lives.

Latest despatches to the State Department indicated today that at least 246 Americans aboard the Athenia.

Ambassador Kennedy at London reported that 101 American citizens boarded the liner at Liverpool and 145 embarked at Glasgow.

Prominent Canadians Aboard.

VICTORIA, Sept. 3.—(CP)—Sir Richard Lake and Lady Lake, of Victoria, are reported by friends here to have been passengers on board the British liner Athenia, torpedoed west of the Hebrides Islands.

Sir Richard is a former Lieutenant Governor of Saskatchewan and a brother of Lieut. General Sir Percy Lake, also of Victoria.

SANTA BARBARA, Calif. Sept. 3.—(P)—Former Senator William G. McAdoo, secretary of the treasury during the Great War, expressed belief tonight the United States may

Concluded on Page 5, Col. 4.

BELGIUM STAYS NEUTRAL.

BRUSSELS, Sept. 3.—Belgium, violation of whose territory by German forces in 1914 brought Great Britain into the last Great War, today communicated to all interested governments a declaration of its neutrality in the present conflict.

Canada Offers Great Britain Every Aid

Premier King Says Great Voluntary Effort To Be Made

Canada brings her co-operation to Great Britain in the struggle now starting voluntarily as a free nation of the British Commonwealth, Prime Minister Mackenzie King said in an address over the Canadian Broadcasting Corporation national network late Sunday.

There was no home and no family in Canada whose fortunes and freedom were not bound up in the struggle now starting said the Prime Minister as he opened a series of four addresses to Canadian radio listeners by cabinet ministers.

He was followed by Labor Minister Rogers who announced a war time crisis and trade board would be set up to regulate trade, prevent profiteering, or undue enhancement of prices and to ensure efficient distribution of necessary commodities during hostilities.

The other speakers were Justice Minister Lapointe who spoke in French to the same effect as the Prime Minister and Pensions Minister Power who delivered Mr. Rogers' message in French.

Nazi Regime to Blame.

Mr. King spoke as follows:

"For months, indeed for years, the shadow of impending conflict in Europe has been ever present. Through these troubled years, no

Concluded on Page 3, Col. 3.

Report Several Ottawa People Aboard Liner

Three Believed Certain on Ill-Fated Liner

Although it was impossible to ascertain early today exactly who was on board the ill-fated Athenia, it was feared at least three were from Ottawa. There also was a possibility that a number of other Ottawa residents had made late bookings on the liner.

Those believed to be on board from Ottawa were:

Harry W. Bramah, 44, of 173 Irving avenue, accountant for the Canadian Broadcasting Corporation.

Miss Phyllis Moss, 24, of 261 O'Connor street, who has been employed in London for some time.

Thomas Graham, 18, 224 Primrose avenue, a cook's helper on the Athenia.

Others who were in England and were reported to be sailing over the week-end were:

Judith Evelyn, step-daughter of G. L. Smallwood, of Perth, Ont.

Dr. R. M. Lowe, 18 Broadway avenue.

Dr. John M. Armstrong.

Dr. F. H. Pete, 31 Crichton street.

Miss Macy Graham, 224 Primrose avenue.

Mrs. James T. Ward, and her 12-year-old son, James Jr., 30 Spadina avenue.

Concluded on Page 5, Col. 5.

Hitler Leaves For Eastern War Front

BERLIN, Sept. 3.—(P)—(via Copenhagen)—Fuehrer Hitler was reported to have started for the East front to join his soldiers shortly after 10 p.m. (5 p.m. E.D.T.) tonight.

Left in Limousine.

The Fuehrer left the chancellery in a limousine with a shaded headlight while the city was in a complete blackout.

The car made its way slowly through the large, mostly silent crowd standing in the dark Wilhelmplatz.

A few in the crowd near the driveway broke through the small police guard and shouted, "Fuehrer command, we follow till death".

The deepest secrecy was maintained as to what part of the front Hitler would visit or how he would travel.

Crowds Wait As Cabinet Meets on Canada's Part in War

Hundreds waited outside the East Block on Sunday morning as Cabinet Council, hurriedly called to a special session, discussed the numerous issues critical of Great Britain's declaration of war.

Never since the Great War years has any meeting of Cabinet attracted such crowds to Parliament Hill. From long before 10 a.m., when the meeting began, people were gathering to watch the arrival of the ministers, and anxious to be on hand should any statement be issued.

Crowd Stays On.

It was later learned that the Prime Minister's statement would be given at 5.30 p.m., but the crowd around the East Block per-

Canadian War Casualties

By The Canadian Press.

Canadians known or believed to have been on the steamship Athenia, torpedoed off Scotland:

Sir Richard Lake and Lady Lake, Victoria.

Mr. and Mrs. Alyn Edwards, Winnipeg.

Mrs. Mary Cowie, Toronto.

William Clare, North Bay.

Mrs. Ethel Thompson, Toronto.

Rev. William Allen, Toronto.

Andrew Allen, Toronto.

Concluded on Page 5, Col. 7.

Ottawa Men Appointed To New Board

Will Make Up Prices and Trade Board

Three Dominion Government officials will form the wartime Prices and Trade Board created to prevent profiteering, Labor Minister Rogers announced Sunday night.

H.B. McKinnon, commissioner of tariff, will be chairman, and the other board members will be David Sim, commissioner of excise, and F.A. McGregor, commissioner of the combines investigation act.

A committee of citizens is also being set up to act with the prices and trade board in an advisory capacity.

The board will have wide powers to halt any attempt at profiteering in foods, fuel and other necessities of life, but many of the powers granted will be held in reserve for use only if profiteering develops on a wide scale.

Powers of Board.

The new board, said the informal statement, "if it should deem it necessary for the prevention of excessive demand or excessive prices in regard to any necessary of life, may license manufacturers or dealers, fix maximum prices, or take steps to require equitable allocation of quantities of goods among distributors and regular distribution to consumers. Such powers would not be exercised, however, without the specific approval of the Governor-in-Council. It is not anticipated that there would be any early necessity for the employment of measures of this type.

"With the passing of this Order-in-Council it is an indictable offence for any person to unduly prevent or lessen the manufacture, supply or distribution of any necessary of life, or to sell or offer for sale any necessary of life at a price higher than is reasonable. The provisions against the offences of charging excessive

Concluded on Page 16, Col. 6.

Many Join Ottawa Units Over Week-end

A desire to be of service to Canada and the Empire swept hundreds of young men into recruiting centres Saturday and Sunday. Even though many applicants were not physically fit they passed through to doctors of the Royal Canadian Army Medical Corps, hoping against hope that they would be taken on strength. Recruiting signs in bold type were placed everywhere.

The 2nd and 51st Batteries have signed up 100 stalwart recruits. The gunners go into barracks at the Coliseum where arrangements to billet them have already been made by the Royal Canadian Engineers.

Sunday morning officers of the

Concluded on Back Page, Col. 3.

Australia Declares War

MELBOURNE, Sept. 3.—(C.P.-Reuters)—Governor General Lord Gowrie signed Australia's declaration of war against Germany tonight.

Earlier Prime Minister Robert Menzie announced that "Australia is at war. Where Britain stands, stand the people of the Empire and of the British world."

New Zealand Offers Support.

LONDON, Sept. 3.—(C.P.-Havas)—It was reported tonight the British Government had received a cable from the New Zealand Government declaring that Dominion would support the Mother Country in the war against Germany. A cable from Wellington repeatedly said the resources at Britain's disposal.

Admiralty Denies Liner Bremen Captured

LONDON, Sept. 3.—(P)—The British Admiralty tonight denied the accuracy of a report picked up by the Mutual Broadcasting System in a short wave broadcast from Paris that the $20,000,000 German liner Bremen had been captured by the British navy. A spokesman for the Admiralty said the report was not true. No word was available, however, as to the ship's position at sea.

Amusement Ads. on Page 3.

Poles Carry Warfare Into Germany

Cavalry Forces German Invaders Back Across Western Frontier

LONDON, Sept. 4.—(Monday)—(P)—An exchange telegraph despatch from Warsaw reported early today Polish troops had crossed the German frontier north of Breslau and were fighting on German soil.

Quoting a Polish short wave radio broadcast, the agency said the troops had crossed between Rawicz and Lessno. These towns are on the border about 25 miles apart and approximately 45 miles north of Breslau.

The report said Polish cavalry was in the action.

WARSAW, Sept. 3.—(C.P.)—Polish armed forces reported signal gains on the land and in the air tonight while German air squadrons for the third successive day bombarded this country's towns and cities.

Civilian Toll Heavy.

Hundreds of civilians were reported killed today, swelling the toll of 1,500 reported killed in raids since Germany invaded Poland Friday.

As the announcement of Great Britain and France's entry into the war sped through the country, a Polish radio communique said that Polish cavalry launched a big attack on German contingents which entered Polish territory and forced the invaders back across the western Polish frontier.

The reports, which did not specify the exact zone of op-

Concluded on Page 2, Col. 4.

War Bulletins

LONDON, Sept. 3.—(P)—Reuters News Agency reported tonight from Shanghai that according to a reliable source Japan has assured Great Britain of its neutrality.

BERLIN, Sept. 3.—(P)—The German official news agency, DNB, announced tonight that the Poles had pierced Vistula river dikes in the region of Tscew near the Danzig border, flooding the lower lands of the Vistula valley. The Germans are in complete possession of Tscew and Danzig.

MOSCOW, Sept. 3.—(P)—The official Soviet Russian broadcast tonight reported German planes bombed Warsaw eight times today.

NICE, France, Sept. 3.—(C.P.-Havas)—France's Italian frontier, which had been closed to Italians seeking to enter France, has been reopened to travellers. It was understood this evening.

Australia Declares War

Sea Outrage Rouses Ottawa

A feeling of horror swept through the crowds on uptown streets late Sunday night as the news came telling of the torpedoing of the passenger steamship Athenia by a German submarine.

The reserve of the day, the calm with which Britain's declaration of war and other momentous happenings had been received was broken. There was a play of emotions on the faces of men and women, emotions of sorrow and

Concluded on Back Page, Col. 8.

King George Calls on Empire To Join Britain in Just War

LONDON, Sept. 3.—(P)—The text of the address of the King to his subjects in all parts of the world today follows:

In this grave hour, perhaps the most fateful in our history, I send to every household of my peoples, both at home and overseas, this message, spoken with the same depth of feeling for each one of you as if I were able to cross your threshold and speak to you myself.

For the second time in the lives of most of us, we are at war.

Over and over again, we have tried to find a peaceful way out

Concluded on Page 2, Col. 6.

Britain's Defenders Are Ready to Fight As War Declared

Prime Minister Tells Of Germany's Refusal to Withdraw Troops by 11 a.m. (English Time) As Demanded by Britain

By J. F. SANDERSON.

LONDON, Sept. 3.—(C.P.)—Great Britain and France went to war with Germany today.

As the fateful news was made known, the King sounded a rallying call to his people scattered throughout the British Empire "to stand calm, firm and united" against Germany's challenge to civilized order in the world.

The King broadcast his message of hope and determination a few short hours after Neville Chamberlain, Great Britain's 70-year-old Prime Minister, announced in a brief, simple statement:

"This country is now at war with Germany."

While Britain's navy, army and air force prepared to co-operate with the military machines of France and Poland in a struggle against Hitlerism and everything it stands for, the quiet voice of their commander-in-chief was addressed to "my people at home and my people across the seas who will make our cause their own."

King Addresses Empire.

Seated alone in his study in Buckingham Palace, dressed in the uniform of an admiral of the fleet, the King addressed this message to every British subject:

"If one and all we keep resolutely faithful to it (the cause), ready for whatever service or sacrifice it may demand, then in God's name we shall prevail."

Shortly afterward it was revealed that members of the Royal Family, as in the Great War, were ready immediately to stand with their subjects in the duties of war.

The Duke of Kent, a simple Admiralty announcement said, has taken a war assignment as a rear-admiral.

The machinery of government was immediately adjusted to war conditions. As predicted the leading figures of the struggle of 1914-18—Winston Churchill and Lord Hankey.

Churchill And Eden Join British Cabinet

LONDON, Sept. 3.—(P)—A war cabinet of nine members to direct Great Britain's struggle against the German Reich was formed by Prime Minister Chamberlain less than five hours after war was declared today.

In the Great War more than two years elapsed before a similar, compact directorate was set up.

Two Great War Figures.

In today's war cabinet Mr. Chamberlain called two of the leading figures of the struggle of 1914-18—Winston Churchill and Lord Hankey.

Mr. Churchill was returned to his old post of First Lord of the Admiralty, which he held before and during the first year of the Great War.

Lord Hankey, who as Sir Maurice Hankey, secretary to the war cabinet, was one of David Lloyd George's right-hand men and was entrusted with many important missions, was made minister without portfolio.

Anthony Eden, former Foreign Secretary, returned to the Government as Secretary of State for the Dominions.

Although not in the war cabinet, he will have special access to the inner group in order that he "may be in the best position to

Concluded on Page 11, Col. 3.

Mr. Churchill was one of four brilliant civil servants, and a confidant of the Prime Ministers since the Great War. He emerged from retirement to enter the ministry. Anthony Eden, former Foreign Secretary, became Secretary for Dominions.

After two weeks of unsuccessful attempts to convince Germany that her territorial claims against Poland should be settled at the conference table, Britain declared war in fulfilment of her pledge to Poland.

Declaration of War.

The actual declaration consisted of R. Dunbar, head of the treaty department of the Foreign Office, notifying Dr. Kordt, Charge d'Affaires.

Concluded on Back Page, Col. 8.

THE WEATHER

TORONTO, Sept. 3.—(P)—Thundershowers have occurred in some parts of Northern Ontario, also light showers in Northern Manitoba, though in other districts east of the Rockies the weather has been generally fair and warm.

Fair and warm in Ontario and somewhat cooler in Manitoba and Saskatchewan.

War News On Inside Pages

For Latest War News see also pages 10, 11 and 18.

BANK STREET BLAZE

Children playing with matches were blamed for a fire which broke out in the back shed of the Belle's Dress Shop, 193 Bank street, on Sunday at 6.25 p.m. Ottawa Fire Department put out the blaze.

44. Three views of the first German magnetic mine to be dismantled.

raiders, and aircraft as well as U-boats. But mines only affected coastal waters where, however, they were menace enough. In November 1939 some 27 ships (121,000 tons) were sunk by them in the approaches to British ports in what the Admiralty described as an attempt to drive neutral countries away from trade with Britain. Fortunately the hazardous dismantling of one magnetic mine, which had been inadvertently dropped by aircraft on a mudbank in the Thames Estuary, revealed its secrets. Effective counter-measures, which took months to implement, included an electrical sweep and the "degaussing" of ships — the neutralizing of their magnetism by placing cables round their hulls and passing current through them.

A Canadian, Charles Frederick Goodeve, had much to do with both the sweep and degaussing. A native of Winnipeg, a gold-medallist of the Engineering Institute of Canada who had joined the Royal Canadian Navy's Volunteer Reserve, Dr. Goodeve was Reader in Physical Chemistry at

45. Commodore Sir Charles Goodeve.

University College, London, when war broke out. He then joined the Royal Naval Volunteer Reserve and was to become Deputy Controller for research and development at the Admiralty and later Commander Sir Charles Goodeve, Vice-Chief of the Naval Staff, Research and Development. He worked closely with Dr. A.B. Wood, chief scientist of the Mine Design Department, RN, who first suggested the demagnetization of ships and how to do it. His method involved coils that were successful but expensive. Goodeve proposed a cheaper and speedier method whereby a long electric cable would be passed around the ship. This came into extensive use, enabling even the smallest ship to be protected. "It was," Goodeve said, "the first technical battle in which we won a decisive victory over the enemy." It was to be followed by many more.

Degaussing gave immediate protection to ships. Could the mines be destroyed, however, that would be better because it would remove the danger. The "Double-L" sweep, a towed magnetic sweep developed by Goodeve, exploded the mines. It was invaluable for sweeping safe channels out of ports and, when the Allies returned to the Continent, for clearing mines from harbour entrances.

Land-based aircraft had limited range — though after the fall of France, Goering's *Luftwaffe*, flying from captured airfields, destroyed thousands of tons of supplies in London's docks. This forced the closing of the Port of London to ocean-going shipping and the diversion of all vessels from there,

as well as from east-coast ports, to Glasgow, Liverpool and Bristol in the West. As a result west-coast port facilities became overstrained, warehouses overloaded, and Britain's internal supply lines disrupted. The turn-round of ships was slowed to the detriment of Britain's lifeline.

Warships and surface raiders took their toll — compensated, for the British, by the sinking of the pocket battleship *Graf Spee*, which had been preying with speed and unpredictability on the shipping lanes. Between 30 September and the first week of December 1939 *Graf Spee* sank nine ships (totalling 50,000 tons), eight of them in the South Atlantic. Harried by three lightly-armed cruisers (no match for the German warship), *Graf Spee* suffered some damage and steamed away from the assailants — which through skilful handling had divided the enemy's fire but had been heavily punished — to effect repairs in the neutral port of Montevideo, Uruguay; the ship anchored on 13 December. Forced by neutrality laws to quit the port after completing repairs, on 17 December *Graf Spee* scuttled herself outside the three-mile limit on the orders of the captain, Hans Langsdorff, who had been misled by British-inspired reports that a large naval force awaited him. In fact there were only three cruisers — two from the original squadron and *Cumberland*, which had replaced the crippled *Exeter*.

Submarines continued to be the most deadly weapon in the German arsenal at sea. The Germans had 57 U-boats at the outbreak of the war; only about a third of them were operational at any one time. Part of the force would be in port for rest or

46. Degaussing-cables in the forepeak of HMCS *St. Stephen* (frigate).

47. *Graf Spee* scuttles herself.

replenishment; another part on the way to or from the killing grounds. The submarines remained in the North Atlantic until the end of March 1940, when they were sent to Norway to help in that campaign. Their score to this point was 185 merchant ships, an aircraft carrier and a battleship. *U-29* torpedoed HMS *Courageous* on 17 September while the carrier was performing anti-submarine patrols in the Western Approaches; she sank in fifteen minutes with the loss of 519 officers and men. On the night of 13 October, under a streaming canopy of northern lights, the battleship HMS *Royal Oak* was sunk at her anchorage at the naval base of Scapa Flow (Orkney Islands) by *U-47*, which, with cool audacity, penetrated the British defences to torpedo the ship; 833 officers and men slid below the surface with her. During this period the Germans lost 15 U-boats, a large proportion of their strength, while only six new boats were commissioned.

Grand Admiral Erich Raeder, head of the German navy, not only wanted the lost boats replaced; he wanted at least 300 with which to

48. HMS *Courageous* keels over before sinking.

1939-1940

49. HMS *Royal Oak*, sunk at Scapa Flow.

50. Raeder.

dominate the Atlantic in 1941. Hitler, deluded by his easy success in France and confident that Britain's fate was also sealed, allocated a mere 5 per cent of steel production to the navy. The result was that for the remainder of 1940 Admiral Karl Doenitz, the U-boat leader, was forced to work with fewer submarines than he had at the beginning of the war.

The British lack of escorts was due to Britain's underestimation of the submarine threat in the inter-war years. Germany had been denied submarines under the terms of the Versailles Treaty and not before 1935 — when the Anglo-German treaty provided for submarine parity — did there seem to be need to build up counter-measures. The London Submarine Protocol of 1936, signed by Germany, outlawed the sinking of unescorted merchant ships without warning, and this, as we have seen, Hitler at first was to honour. It would be naive, however, to think that Britain had complete faith in Hitler; destroyers were fitted for anti-submarine tasks. But too much reliance was placed on asdic (the device produced by the *A*llied *S*ubmarine *D*etection *I*nvestigation *C*ommittee — the Americans called it sonar — which, by the reflection of sound impulses from submerged

51. The asdic set; officer and operator, aboard a
Canadian corvette, listen intently.

objects, could determine the direction and distance
of submarines), and this proved useless against
surfaced boats. These were hard to see at night.
Radar small enough to be fitted in small ships had
not been developed at this stage of the war.

Confident that asdic would effectively outlaw the
kind of ruthless submarine warfare that had been
such a dangerous feature of the First World War,
the Admiralty — which was preoccupied with
Hitler's emerging "big ship" navy — turned, after
1936, to the building of five new battleships, six
aircraft carriers and 19 heavy and light cruisers at
the expense of smaller escorts. The primary role of
destroyers, in the thinking of the day, was the
support of capital ships. Thus few destroyers were
available for anti-submarine warfare when war
broke out. Instead of screening convoys closely,
many of these destroyers were at first wasted on
anti-U-boat sweeps of trade routes — sweeps that
were usually abortive, for if a destroyer was seen on
the horizon the U-boat submerged — deeply — and
kept quiet until the destroyer passed on. Yet sweeps
did bring some rewards: in March 1940, for
example, the Canadian destroyer *Assiniboine*
(acquired from Britain in October 1939)* and a
British cruiser captured the German merchant ship
Hannover, a valuable prize that became the *Empire*

*Her captain, Commander Rollo Mainguy, was to become
Vice-Admiral, Chief of the Naval Staff, in the post-war years.

Audacity and, when converted, joined the Royal
Navy as the auxiliary aircraft carrier HMS
Audacity. The encounter took place on the coast of
The Dominican Republic and was full of drama.
The British cruiser stopped the German ship, whose
crew then set it on fire. By the time the Canadian
destroyer arrived, the blazing merchantman, with
steering gear smashed, was drifting into the safety
of neutral waters. *Assiniboine* secured a line and
towed the vessel seaward. For four days, taking
turns at hosing and towing the smouldering
merchantman, the two naval ships struggled with

52. HMCS *St. Laurent*.

1939-1940

53. A transatlantic convoy from the air.

the yawing vessel through rising seas until, securing themselves to the prize to port and starboard, they edged their victim into harbour at Kingston, Jamaica. This was exciting work, but it was carried out at the expense of escort duty.

Britain had only 180 ships fitted with asdic at the outbreak of war, 150 of them destroyers. With the majority of these assigned to the protection of the fleet, a score of older destroyers, a handful of sloops and a few anti-submarine trawlers were all that were available for convoy duties; rarely could more than two escorts be provided for any convoy.

Canada's destroyers were helpful at this stage of

the war. There were only six of them, *Ottawa, Fraser, Restigouche, St. Laurent, Saguenay* and *Skeena*. The first four had been on the West Coast, but with news of impending war *Fraser* and *St. Laurent* were quickly dispatched, via Panama, to Halifax. Six days after Canada declared war the first wartime convoy sailed from Halifax escorted by three of the destroyers. Minesweepers, part of Canada's fleet of five, swept the channel outside the harbour's mouth while obsolescent flying boats of the Royal Canadian Air Force flew ahead to look for the tell-tale feather caused by a U-boat's raised periscope. The pattern that was subsequently followed was thus established. Far out to sea, at the limit of their endurance, other Stranraer aircraft that had taken over the patrol would flash "goodbye and good luck!" by Aldis lamp and turn for home. The merchantmen and their escorts were on their own. Long before mid-ocean was reached the naval escorts would turn back, escorting a westbound convoy, leaving the merchant ships to make their way alone or with a single armed merchant-cruiser (usually a converted passenger liner) for escort. (One such ship, the British *Jervis Bay*, encountered the pocket battleship *Admiral Scheer* on a crossing in November 1940. *Jervis Bay* ordered the convoy

54. Troops of the 1st Canadian Division, bound for Britain, board the Canadian Pacific liner *Empress of Britain* at Halifax, December 1939.

to scatter and then deliberately steamed within range of the enemy's 11-inch guns until she herself, with her weaker armament, could strike the enemy. Punished all the way, by that time she was a blazing wreck. But she worked her guns and by engaging her adversary gave the ships in the convoy time to escape. Thanks to her self-sacrifice, only four ships out of 37 were sunk). Then air patrols and naval escort would pick up the convoy in the dangerous Western Approaches to the British Isles.

At the start of the war convoy escort fully occupied Canada's tiny navy. Canadian destroyers helped escort the 1st Canadian Division to England at the end of 1939. The defence of Canada's enormous coastline had to be left to the Fishermen's Reserve with 15 suitable vessels drawn from British Columbia's fishing fleet; and to yachts that were requisitioned, armed, manned by RCN crews, and used for anti-submarine patrols in eastern waters. Yachts were lost: *Otter* in 1941 through fire; *Raccoon* in 1942, probably by torpedo, though not one of her company of four officers and 34 men survived to say. The destruction, or preferably capture, of enemy merchant ships — a vital task — was left to three fast liners, taken over in the winter of 1939-40 from Canadian National Steamships, converted to armed merchant cruisers and commissioned as HMC Ships *Prince Robert, Prince Henry* and *Prince David. Prince Robert*, in September 1940, captured the German merchantman *Weser*, with a valuable cargo, off the

coast of Mexico; the ship joined Canada's merchant fleet as the *Vancouver Island. Prince Henry* attempted to capture the freighter *Muenchen* off Peru, but the ship set herself on fire, as did a second, *Hermonthis*, shortly afterwards. Both sank but were lost to Germany. Even one of Canada's minesweepers, *Bras d'Or*, captured a ship, shortly after Italy's entry into the war; the *Capo Noli* also entered Canadian merchant service. *Bras d'Or* foundered in a raging gale in the Gulf of St. Lawrence four months later, her crew going down with her.

The destroyers' escort tasks were dramatically interrupted in June 1940, when it became imperative to evacuate British troops (and the French who desired it) from France. *Fraser* sank, sliced in two in a nighttime collision with a British cruiser; *Restigouche* rescued all but forty of her crew. It was Canada's first naval disaster of the war. In all, 338,000 British and French soldiers were successfully withdrawn, almost all from Dunkirk, though it had been predicted that no more than 45,000 could be got away. But to save the men, artillery, vehicles and ammunition had to be abandoned. There were virtually disarmed soldiers, of little use for counter-invasion until re-equipped, and Britain faced the task of making the losses good.

Britain's position deteriorated rapidly and disastrously with the fall of France, not only through the loss of the equipment of her army. A vast arc of coastline, from Norway to the Spanish

55. HMCS *Prince Robert*.

56. HMCS *Restigouche* at Plymouth, June 1940. Ahead are *Skeena* and *St. Laurent*.

57. Crew members of *Restigouche* at Plymouth just before leaving for the coast of France.

58. HMCS *Fraser*, lost 25 June 1940 after colliding with HMS *Calcutta* during the evacuation of troops from St. Jean-de-Luz, France.

border, had turned hostile almost overnight, giving Germany better bases from which to fight the Atlantic war. Behind that coastline were Hitler's successful armies, rich in armour, waiting to invade. The German air arm, far stronger than Britain's, now had fields across the Channel, within easy striking distance, from which to support a seaborne invasion. Britain had lost the support of the French fleet; the Italian fleet had ranged itself on the side of Germany. The Mediterranean was closed to British merchant shipping, as were the ''short-haul'' Continental ports; supply lines lengthened. What British troops could be sent (and Churchill took the risk) to the Mediterranean and East Africa to counter Mussolini's legions in his African empire had to go all the way around the Cape.

Hitler, convinced that Britain's situation was hopeless after the fall of France, sought peace. He confidently expected that his last-remaining opponent's nerve would crack. Prime Minister Churchill rallied the British people to fight to the end and the Commonwealth stood with them. With no response to his peace overtures Hitler ordered preparations for invasion, finally setting the date for mid-September. Reconnaissance aircraft brought ominous reports of enemy concentrations of shipping of all types assembled in ports from Oslo to Brest; large concentrations of troops and transport were observed; and the enemy, with his usual thoroughness, was seen to be carrying out embarkation and landing exercises along the Channel coast.

Germany was strong on the ground and in the air but weak by sea; in fact the German navy remained skeptical about Hitler's invasion plans. But if the Royal Air Force could be destroyed, a seaborne invasion would be a practicable operation, for it would be protected from British naval interference by the *Luftwaffe* — a vast air umbrella that would shelter the invading forces. An essential preliminary to the invasion of Britain, therefore, was the destruction of the Royal Air Force. During July, as part of the softening-up process, German aircraft attacked shipping in the Channel and Britain's southern ports.

In the Battle of Britain, which followed, the Royal Air Force and its Commonwealth and Allied contingents scored a decisive victory. On 17 September Hitler, despairing on a September crossing and with the weather deteriorating in the fall, postponed the invasion indefinitely. He ordered the dispersal of invasion craft and troop concentrations in the Channel ports to avoid the British bombing attacks to which they had been subjected.

Throughout this period the Royal Navy had to be prepared to repel invasion from the sea, no matter what the punishment might be, or the cost. It was the most vital task if Britain were to survive and it had first priority. That included destroyers, withdrawn from convoy work for the evacuation of troops from France and held for the defence of Britain. Canadian destroyers, which had been in action against U-boats, but with no conclusive results, were also held until the end of July, when

59. Invasion barges, massed in Boulogne harbour, from the air.

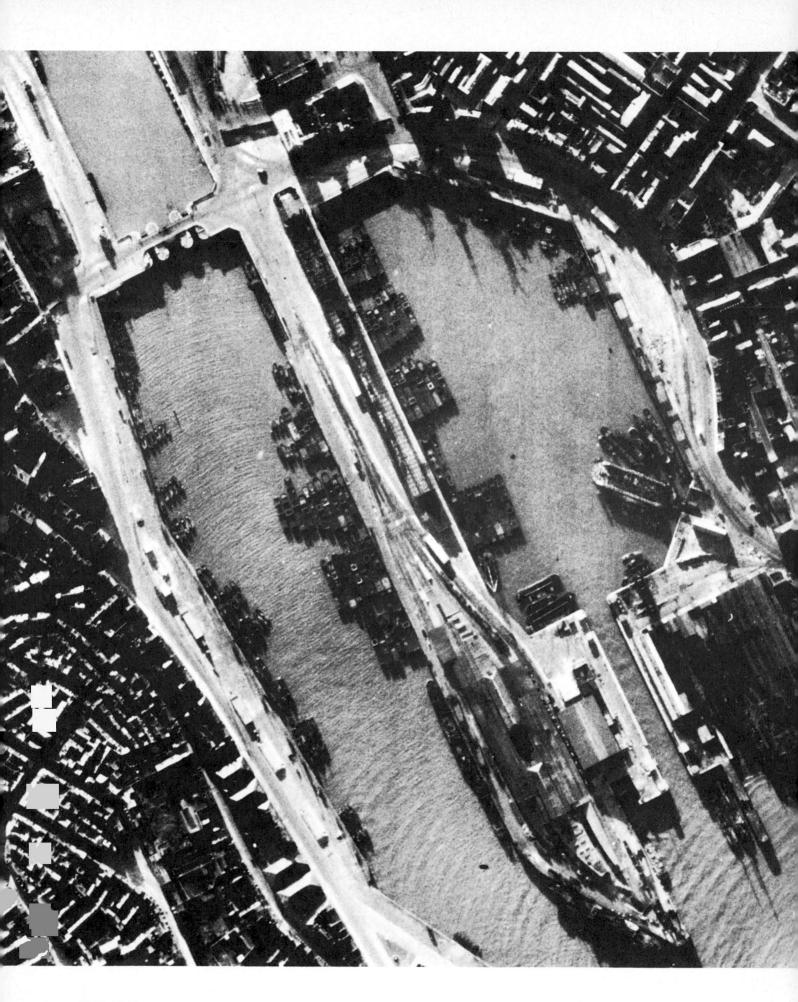

60. HMCS *Columbia*, one of the over-age U.S. destroyers acquired by Canada. She is seen here towing a badly-damaged British destroyer (HMS *Caldwell*) to Halifax.

they joined the Northern Escort Force in Scotland.

Escorts, then, were desperately needed, and it was fortunate that Churchill was able to persuade Roosevelt to part with 50 old destroyers — ships that had their faults but which could be used for escort work — in exchange for leases of British bases in Newfoundland and the Caribbean. Canada acquired six of these four-funnelled ships in September — *Annapolis, Columbia, Niagara, St. Clair, St. Croix, St. Francis;* and *Hamilton* later. She also acquired a British replacement for *Fraser*, HMCS *Margaree*. But like her predecessor, this destroyer was sunk through collision — on 21 October while escorting a small convoy to Halifax. Only 31 survived out of 171 officers and men.

To provide close escorts for the fleet of 3,000 oceangoing merchant ships on which Britain's survival depended had never proved possible. The British continued to protect convoys from home ports only as far as a line about 200 miles west of

61. Another ex-US destroyer, HMCS *St. Croix*, heavily damaged by a hurricane in December 1940.

1939-1940

Ireland (longitude 15°W). From there ships dispersed or had the protection of only an armed merchant cruiser; the practice was the same from Canadian ports. It was soon found that U-boats could range beyond that line to sink individual merchant ships or those that were insufficiently protected. Consequently, ships were escorted to a line farther out (longitude 17°W), which stretched the provision of escorts to the limit. Still the sinkings continued, for now the Germans had Norwegian bases, and those on the coast of France lengthened the range of U-boat operations.

Aircraft could have helped. U-boats relied, when submerged, upon electric motors powered by huge batteries; they had to surface for several hours each day so that the main diesel engines, which required air, could be used to recharge the batteries. Air attack at such times would either destroy the U-boat or force it down — interrupting the recharging period and seriously interfering with the boat's operations. But though Coastal Command of the RAF was established, its aircraft were of modest range. Bomber Command had priority for aircraft of longer range, and these were to be busily employed against German towns and industries while U-boats sank Allied ships with impunity. In view of the results, priorities could well have been reversed.

Other factors weighed against Britain in these early months. She no longer possessed bases on the west coast of Ireland, bases which had been of great use in the earlier war. Though Britain still supplied Eire by sea, carrying goods through air and U-boat attacks at great cost, that country had declared neutrality, and the three naval bases in southern Ireland were denied to Britain and her Allies for offensive operations. Britain gained one advantage after the German occupation of Denmark in the spring of 1940 when she, in turn, occupied Iceland — an independent state under the King of Denmark* — to keep the strategic island out of German hands. The benefit was not immediate, but the move enabled Britain to develop naval and air bases in this vital area at a later date.

Much of the French fleet, on which Britain had counted through alliance with France, was lost. And when Italy entered the war in mid-June, Mussolini put 26 modern submarines at the disposal of the Germans, while Britain's obsession with Italy meant that shipping and escorts were consumed in sending supplies to Egypt and or East Africa round the Cape. In December the Canadian destroyer, *Saguenay*, was torpedoed by an Italian submarine. Her survival was seldom repeated when other

*During the war normal communications between Iceland and Denmark ceased. The union, which expired in January 1944, was not renewed. Iceland proclaimed itself a republic in June.

62. Following the German invasion of Denmark in April, 1940 the British occupied Iceland, strategically situated in the North Atlantic. Canadian troops helped garrison the island. Some are shown encamped here, near Reykjavik.

escorts were similarly attacked, and accounts of the action demonstrate how lethal even a single torpedo could be.

63. The damaged bow of HMCS *Saguenay*, after being torpedoed by the Italian submarine *Argo* on 1 December, 1940. Though the forepart of the ship was lost, she managed to reach the British port of Barrow-in-Furness five days later.

64. German propaganda mocks de Gaulle's abortive attack on Dakar.

The shock of the exploding torpedo, which blew a gaping hole in the bows, was followed almost immediately by raging flames close to the magazine. Within minutes the ship was "a red hot coal in the middle of a pitchblack ocean." Yet men carried the ammunition to safety, switched off the ventilating fans and ran out hoses; by dawn the fire, though smouldering and every now and then erupting, had been brought under control. *Saguenay* was, however, low in the water in rough weather. Her captain, Lieutenant-Commander George Miles, brought her into harbour after a 4½-day battle against the sea. Casualties included 21 dead and 18 injured from wounds and burns.

There were reasons to hang on in North Africa and the Mediterranean. It was one region where Axis forces could be directly engaged; and it was essential not to abandon Middle Eastern oil supplies. Additionally, Churchill hoped to win French West Africa, which would protect the Gibraltar gateway, through de Gaulle. But a seaborne attack on Dakar by Free French forces in September 1940 proved abortive; it merely increased Vichy French hostility and did much to discredit de Gaulle, who had suggested it. The British hoped, in the long run, to break into the continent of Europe from North Africa, a far less hazardous enterprise than invading North-West Europe across the English Channel. In 1940, though, they came close to losing the Battle of the Atlantic because of their determination to hold as much as they could in the Mediterranean theatre.

Quick to take advantage of their improved position, the Germans, as early as July 1940, attacked shipping, generally in the approaches to the western ports, with every submarine that could be made available. That month HMCS *St. Laurent* rescued more than 800 oil-soaked passengers from the torpedoed liner *Arandora Star*. The U-boats operated singly, usually by day, finding their own targets and sinking ships by torpedoes when submerged; or by gunfire from the surface, if the ship was an independently-sailing defenceless merchantman. With the greater part of the destroyer flotillas concentrated for anti-invasion tasks, there was little the British could do. A convoy covering ten square miles often had no more protection than could be provided by a couple of anti-submarine trawlers. From July to the end of October was the ''happy time'' for U-boats. They sank over a million tons of shipping — an average of over 9,000 tons a day, the highest success rate of the whole war. These deadly operations forced the British, in October 1940, to escort ships to a line even farther out (longitude 19°W) — which stretched the provision of escorts still more despite new corvettes (small escorts) coming into service. The sinkings continued, for in August Doenitz had decided to change tactics.

He remembered his own experience when

65. A "happy time" for U-boats. "They sank over a million tons of shipping."

66. A U-boat points its deckgun at a freighter. (overleaf)

67. A "wolf-pack" moves out to sea.

commanding a U-boat in the First World War — that a submarine on the surface at night is almost invisible; and that, using its diesel engines, it can travel fast. He himself had penetrated a convoy's screen of escorts, had moved in amongst the merchant ships and calmly sunk more than one before making his escape at speed on the surface or by submerging. Suppose several U-boats were concentrated to attack the same convoy together, on the same night? The execution would be indescribable and the few escorts would be powerless to prevent it. To locate the convoy he decided to stretch a picket line of U-boats across the main shipping routes; the first U-boat to spot a convoy would report to U-boat headquarters by radio — communications were good — and headquarters in turn would concentrate the U-boats. He thus introduced ''wolf pack'' tactics in the late summer of 1940, so successfully that U-boat operations were based on them for the next three years. They were aided, from late 1940, by long-range FW200 (Condor) aircraft that would spot and report a convoy; U-boat headquarters would then order the U-boats to close on the reported position as before. During three nights alone in October, 38 ships were lost from three convoys to ''wolf pack'' tactics.

Sinkings for 1940 amounted to 3,991,641 tons, all but 300,000 in the North Atlantic (755,392 had been lost in 1939). U-boats claimed the greatest score, 2,186,158 versus 580,074 for aircraft; 509,889 for mines; 511,615 for surface warships and armed raiders; and 203,905 attributed to other causes. Six German raiders had put out to sea in the spring of 1940 — ships that had the appearance of peaceful merchantmen but which carried guns and torpedo tubes; some had aircraft to increase their reach. They alone sank or captured half a million tons of shipping (most of it on the remoter trade routes) by the end of 1941, when they themselves had been either sunk or driven from the seas.

At the end of 1940, 606 ships had been lost since the war began. As Britain had started the war with about 3,000 (2,000 fewer than she had possessed at the end of the First World War, though her population had increased by about 4 million since then), she had lost about one-fifth of her merchant fleet. This was far more than British shipyards, which had to cope with damaged vessels, could replace by new construction. Only 16 U-boats had been sunk since April, and 50 had been commissioned.

68. Used at first for long-range maritime patrols and bombing, the chief role of the Condor soon became the reporting of convoys and directing of U-boat packs to them.

69 & 70. The losses of ships, and their cargoes, mounted.

71. Fog

There were many reasons for this disaster, apart from the lack of escorts. One was weather — we have seen the tonnage lost from "other causes." Britain's North Atlantic lifeline passes through some of the worst weather in the world. It is subject to fog for days on end, especially on the Newfoundland Banks, and to summer gales that build the sea to enormous heights of 60 feet and more. Even in peacetime crossings are hazardous; for wartime convoys much more so. Ships collided in the fog, or simply foundered in heavy seas. Periods of sunny calm — a welcome respite in normal times, and not infrequent — came to be dreaded when U-boats ranged the Atlantic wastes, for good visibility and smooth seas made torpedo strikes more likely. Such days, of course, gave patrolling airmen the edge over U-boats, but air cover was negligible in the opening years of the Atlantic battle. Winter, for seamen and airmen alike, was a nightmare. Waves breaking over ships and flying spray turned to ice that encrusted superstructures so thickly that foundering and capsizing from its weight was possible. Aircraft iced up in the freezing air and their coastal bases were either frozen or blotted out by snow. The weather favoured U-boats, which even when surfaced were hard to spot in rough seas; and ice, to them, was generally not a problem for they could submerge.

Furthermore the opposing weapons-systems — the torpedo versus the asdic/depth-charge combination — again favoured the U-boat. The swift torpedo, aimed at a *seen* ship, was obviously more deadly than the escorts' groping reach to an unseen target. Asdic, in any case, was imprecise. Turbulence — natural, or caused by explosions or a ship's propeller — affects sound waves much as rain interrupts light waves in the air. Variations in water temperature also affect sound; asdic was almost useless in the Arctic. Nor could it detect a submarine on the surface. It would be some time yet before radar small enough to be installed in corvettes or in aircraft became available. The depth charge, a 250-pound drum of explosives projected over the suspected position of a U-boat (with its fuse pre-set to explode at the submarine's estimated depth) was equally imprecise. To sink its quarry, the charge had to explode within 20 feet of the U-boat's sturdy hull. This was difficult to achieve when the submarine was able to slip sideways or down, and a U-boat captain soon became skilled in evasion.

The paramount reason for Britain's extreme vulnerability at the end of 1940, however, was of course the fall of France. That a nation, so strong on paper, could crumble so quickly had never been foreseen. It left British plans in tatters, both on land and by sea, and improvisation had to serve in circumstances that had changed so drastically.

72. Storm

73. Breaking seas

74. Calm

1939-1940

75. Ice

76. The Women's Land Army, which freed men for service, cuts down food imports. By 1944 it had 200,000 members.

voyages. Two Canadian tunnelling companies (engineers) mined mineral deposits in Britain. These were of importance to the munitions industry and, again, cut down imports. The engineers also supplied extra water to a bauxite plant in Scotland by means of a two-mile tunnel cut through solid rock. This made it possible to step up the supply of aluminum, required for aircraft production. But most of this was for the future and, though useful, it was not a major factor in terms of Britain's total imports. The situation was desperate at the end of 1940.

In the eight months from the outbreak of the war to the invasion of Norway (September 1939 – April 1940) a couple of hundred merchant ships had been lost for 17 U-boats sunk, a ratio that was not insupportable. During the next eight months, peaking after the loss of France, the British lost twice that number of ships and accounted for fewer U-boats. This was a rate she could not long endure.

Britain was losing the "tonnage war". As early as January 1940 ham, bacon, butter and sugar were restricted to four ounces per adult per week, and the ration was to be further reduced. Less than three weeks' supply of wheat remained, and reserves of raw materials had fallen to a dangerous level — for example, a two weeks' stock of iron ore. In December 1939 every available ship had been ordered to North America for wheat; it would then be the turn of the Ministry of Supply for iron ore. Iron railings around parks in London and elsewhere were torn down for melting. The Womens' Land Army working on the farms, and the raising of vegetables in parks, gardens, and in "allotments" on uncultivated land halved food imports. An "eat more potatoes" campaign led to a 60 per cent increase in this home-produced commodity, and it was the same with carrots. Britain was to become self-sufficient in vegetables, and food imports were cut from two-thirds of her total requirements to one-third by the end of 1941. The salvage of waste paper, scrap metal, even collections of pots and pans, saved imports. Canadian Army forestry companies, the first of which started work in the winter of 1940 and which were to increase to 20 (a peak of 7,000 men in February 1943), cut down trees and produced timber in Britain to reduce imports. The timber produced by each company was estimated to be equivalent to that which could be carried by a ship of 6,000 tons making regular deliveries from Canada through slow wartime

77. Timber! Men of the Canadian Forestry Corps cut down trees in Scotland.

1939-1940

The ship that won the war

Britain had foreseen the shortage of escorts that became so marked in 1940, and she had begun to do something about it when every sign, after Munich, pointed to the inevitability of war.

In March 1938, Hitler's growing belligerence forced the Admiralty to consider the serious lack of escort vessels, and in the spring of 1939 the imminence of war panicked the government into authorizing funds for 56 special escorts; a crash programme for "Flower Class" corvettes began in British shipyards just before the war. Churchill, upon becoming First Lord of the Admiralty in September 1939, added another 30 and ordered still others from Canada (Canada built 54 for her own navy; the 10 built for the Royal Navy were lent to Canada for the duration of the war). Eventually 288

were built. Of course none were available in the early months; the first two of the steady stream of Canadian-built corvettes to be built, for example, were not commissioned until the end of October 1940.

Canadian General A.G.L. McNaughton, when president of the National Research Council, had visited Britain in 1939 and brought back with him blueprints of war material he considered might be built in Canada, incuding corvettes. The construction of corvettes and Bangor-class minesweepers in Canada was authorized in early 1940. For Canadians who manned them, the corvette was the ship that won the Atlantic war. Only one, *Sackville* (the subject of Alan Easton's

78. HMCS *Sackville*.

79. "They were not much to look at"; HMCS *Battleford* in silhouette.

fine book, *50 North*), is still in Canadian service at the time of writing; it is hoped that this ship, if there is any sense of history in the country, will be preserved.

The corvette, designed on the pattern of a whaler, could be produced quickly and cheaply. It was not much to look at. A couple of hundred feet long and broad — a 33-foot beam — the ship provided little more than a floating platform for depth charges and a 4-inch gun mounted on the fo'c'sle. Her mast, unlike that of any other naval ship, was smack in front of the bridge, with a squat funnel behind it. With a crew of 60 odd men, the mess-decks were intolerably crowded — seamen, stokers, signalmen, telegraphists lumped together — so that men had to eat in the sleeping spaces. It was said that a corvette would roll in a heavy dew; they certainly did that in Atlantic waters.

There was as yet no organized programme for "working-up" Canadian ships, which were bound to have a high proportion of new men in their companies as the war progressed; it came with the commissioning of corvettes. And it was important. Through it officers learned their business; individual men of different temperaments, crowded together, became a working team able to do, almost automatically, what was expected of them. Thus the ship came alive, tuned for action. Very generally this was the process.

There had always been drill ashore, and training

The Ship That Won the War

courses in the seamanship, asdic, gunnery, depth-charge and signal departments. But men had to get used to the ship, for inexperienced hands can easily be washed overboard or hurt. Even on the first trips out of harbour they found that a corvette managed to achieve a 30-degree roll in a less than moderate sea, causing damage to moveable gear below decks; they heard the creaking and groaning of the ship, the crash of objects that were flung about — properly stowed but not secured against the weather. That was another lesson. They learned when to hold on — what swinging objects to avoid, especially the boats. Though at least one boat should be kept swung out in wartime, ready to be lowered quickly in an emergency, that was not practicable; corvettes were too lively.

The men suffered seasickness, with its cold sweat, nausea, dizziness and weakness at the knees. It was especially bad in the engine room, where grimy engineers, and stokers bare to the waist, toiled in a reek of stale steam and oil under naked electric light bulbs in wire cages.

Boats were lowered, rowed and hoisted; the hand lead swung for soundings. Men put out mock fires and were taught lookout-keeping. They learned

80. HMCS *Brandon* in harbour.

how to handle the guns in a choppy sea; how to throw depth charges, to read a swinging compass, and compensate with the wheel. They were taught to stoke the furnaces without belching giveaway smoke; the hoisting of signals; and how to use

81. Stoking a corvette.

radar, once ships were fitted with it, so that merchant ships and surfaced U-boats could be "seen." Though the principles had been explained ashore, the familiarity of routine did not come easily at sea, where the unsteady motion of wet decks and cramped quarters affected both mind and stomach.

The "loading number" of the 4-inch gun, for example, might lose the swing when ramming the shell home, leaving the shell half in and half out of the breech; it would have to be extracted. Thus the whole rhythm of firing would be lost — bad enough in training, but in the tearing swells of the North Atlantic a failure to fire might be fatal.

The depth-charge crews found it easy to lose control of heavy, cylindrical objects in a rolling ship. Fuses had to be properly set for the depth required, and the explosive drums unlashed. The throwers were loaded at high speed — a back-breaking job that required teamwork; and the crews might be made up, not only of seamen, but of off-watch stokers and telegraphists who were trained in this as well as in their regular duties.

A raw officer had his first experience of watch-keeping, an unnerving business, especially at night. He was on the bridge, with lookouts to port and starboard, a signalman and asdic rating to share the four-hour watch. He had a voice-pipe to the quartermaster waiting in the wheelhouse for the helm-orders that he would give. By leaning over the bridge rail he could see the whole forepart of the ship, the mast above him rolling against the sky. Below was the sweating hull, dividing 60 men from the sea. He was the focal point of a steady, surging progress, the man who used the engines, altered course and speed, and checked the position of buoys, or a lighthouse perhaps, against the chart in the asdic house. He acquired confidence from these brief periods when the ship was entrusted to his care, and left his fears behind as the ship did its roiling wake.

Finally came the work-ups and trials that the ship must pass at the naval base at Tobermory in the Hebrides, opened in July 1940 (and there was to be one at St. Margaret's Bay, near Halifax, Nova Scotia). Exercises with a submarine, gun drill or running through "action stations" while in harbour, raising the anchor by hand, lowering the boats. Drills and lectures for some; then, with half the ship's company absent, a sudden order that called for the other half to tackle the nearest job, no

82. Canadian recruits learn to load the 4-inch gun.

The Ship That Won the War

83. A loaded depth charge thrower ready for firing. The 300-lb. depth charge has been lifted onto the carrier which fits the barrel of the thrower; a propellant cartridge inside the barrel, when fired, will hurl carrier and depth charge over the side of the ship where the carrier will fall away with the depth charge going on to sink and explode at a pre-set depth.

matter what the men's ratings. Seamen would find themselves hoisting signals, stokers firing guns, telegraphists and coders connecting filthy pipes to take in oil. The aim — alertness and a disciplined reaction in time of crisis that might save all their lives.

At sea they tried out the asdic gear. They tried to perfect the teamwork between asdic operators, the captain and the depth-charge crews that would be vital to success. The hunts themselves, with a submarine for quarry, was what it was all about. They heard the metallic ''ping-ping-ping'' of the asdic echo-sounder, working horizontally around the ship as it reached out for its elusive target, the throb of engines, the tense commands. The ship had to be handled; the submarine had to be both found and held while the corvette ran in; engine revolutions had to be adjusted; signals hoisted (to warn merchantmen and other escorts); the depth-charge crews alerted; and the right handle pressed at the right time. There were, at first, a depressing number of failures, but with time and practice the drill improved. The idiosyncracies of the ship and its asdic became familiar, as did the

84. A depth charge, the main anti-submarine weapon, explodes.

85. Almost engulfed, HMCS *Swansea* (frigate) ploughs through heavy seas, as does another escort.

anticipation of what a hunted U-boat might do to evade detection. They picked up the submarine — and held it — down to the mock ''kill.'' The corvette, through the increasing skill of its company, had become a working proposition. The ship went on from there to practice with other corvettes so that each could make an effective contribution without getting in the others' way.

Veterans of corvettes and frigates (twin-screw corvettes) have their memories of convoy escort duty: of the utter discomfort of the crossings in gales and heavy seas; the shriek of the wind in taut wires — the crash and pounding of the waves; the groans of the ship as it swung with slanting decks over the precipice from crest to trough, then paused — as if unable to recover — and finally climbed, by a miracle, it seemed, to the crest of the next enormous sea. At one moment the ship was buried; then the famous whaler design took over and the

bows rose, shedding the torrents of water that had roared over the decks and filled the passageways. Free, and crazily riding the crest amid the wind and sheets of glistening spray, the next plunge would follow until the bows again dug deep into the oncoming sea. Men were sick, wet and cold for days on end and the mess-decks stank of vomit. They recall the wallowing merchant ships, trying hard to keep their stations, streaming white water down rust-caked sides. And above, the low, tearing clouds.

There were, of course, the calmer days after the wind had dropped to end the shrieking and make audible the sound of steadily-pounding engines and light creaks and moans as the vessel rolled. The stars shone between higher clouds on a sea that tumbled, but one which had lost the angry whitecaps that had swept, one after the other, in mounting fury to engulf the ship.

Off-watchmen, wedged between the tops of lockers and the deck-head in the lively ships, slept

The Ship That Won the War

the sleep of the weary. Others, still in wet clothes, slept in slung hammocks. Clothes remained on all through voyages and men looked forward to showers, clean sheets and hot meals at the terminal ports.

When head-on gales persisted, convoys made little progress. Fresh food ran out, first milk and bread, then meat and vegetables. Salt cod, corned beef and ship biscuit were often the only food available towards the end of a bad crossing. Escorting a slow convoy (six knots in good weather) could take three weeks and more. A captain escorting a westbound convoy might order the discharge of a single depth-charge in the fish-rich waters off Newfoundland. Literally hundreds of fish would rise to float, belly up, at the site of the explosion. Leaving the mangled fish at the centre to the wheeling, screaming, demented gulls, the ship's boat loaded up with slippery fresh cod at the rim of the circle, where they were unmarked and merely stunned. That night a man ate all he could.

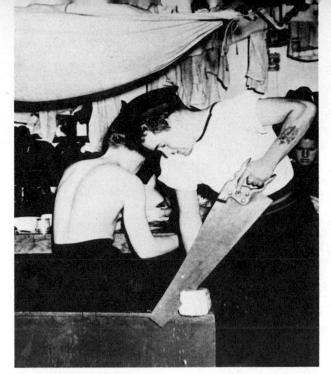

86. A sailor cuts stale bread; above, his shipmate sleeps in a slung hammock.

87. "Men were wet and cold for days on end. . . ."

Winter brought further miseries, and not only at sea. There was St. John's which Canadian corvettes began to use in May 1941, with its heavy falls of snow. Men floundered through it, carrying aboard supplies of food, depth-charges and ammunition; they cleared piles of the stuff over the side of the ship into the dark waters of the harbour. Then there was ice — not so much the pack ice that covered the sea, especially off Newfoundland, but the icing of the ships themselves (though fortunately it was a rare occurrence).

Flying spray, caused by breaking seas, froze in bitter weather and coated the ships with ice. With

88. Crew members of HMCS *Kamsack* (corvette) eat sauerkraut and sausages in calm weather.

every successive wave the crust thickened, so that everything above the waterline, including the foremast, was soon encased in solid ice; even steel wires became shimmering, brittle cables the size of a man's thigh. The weight was enormous. Crew-members, even officers — chilled to the bone — swung at the ice with axes or whatever they could find. It was a race against time and no man could be spared. Their best hope was for the storm to abate, for new ice often formed faster than the old could be broken away. In cross-seas, when the build-up took place on one side or the other, it was worse, for then the ship would list and the response to the helm would be clumsy and erratic, making it hard — as was often possible — to struggle into the lee of land and shelter from the wind and spray. Ships that failed to rid themselves of the massive loads of ice foundered or capsized.

Veterans remember the deadly U-boat attacks, starting in the fall of 1940, when three or four boats attacked almost simultaneously, manoeuvring on the surface in the lanes between the convoy columns, picking their targets at leisure and with care; the dull thuds of detonating torpedoes that followed each other from every quarter; the merchantmen, carrying ore, that sank like stones; the tankers flashing into a roaring holocaust to outline, in stark silhouette, ships sinking and others plodding forward like patient leviathans to escape; the feeling of helplessness that prompted escorts, with no asdic contact, to fire star-shell in hope of

89. Ice was a terror that had to be contended with — an iced-over corvette.

The Ship That Won the War

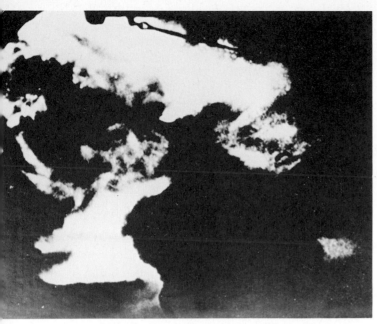

90. "Tankers flashed into a roaring holocaust" as did ammunition ships, such as this.

91. More than one depth charge often brought results; here HMCS *Saguenay* (destroyer) launches two.

spotting a target within gun-range. Improved tactics, whereby every escort fired star-shell simultaneously when a convoy was subjected to wolf pack attack (thus forcing the U-boats to

submerge), were introduced by Lieutenant-Commander K.L. Dyer when captain of the Canadian destroyer *Skeena*. They were effective and widely used.

They remember, too, searching for survivors; the finding of them, with the dead, in pools of stinking

92. "Worse, for submariners, was the suspense of a long hunt."

oil; and the man Canadian Alan Easton describes — in his book *50 North* — who, though dead, still clung to a lifebuoy in a light sea that moved his legs to make him appear to be feebly swimming. They saw the flotsam — lumber by the acre, parts of deckhouses, ladders and the pathetic remnants of cargoes freed from ships that had been ripped apart.

Sometimes U-boats *were* surprised on the surface during these attacks and escorts dashed towards them. Submarines crash-dived, but not all managed to escape the pattern of depth-charges, set for shallow detonation, that plummeted after them. Sometimes a faint red glow, lasting for seconds, was seen below the dark surface; debris bobbed up,

even bodies, floating in a spreading sheet of diesel oil. But worse for submariners was the suspense of a long hunt, after being forced down, during which the "ping" of the probing asdic could be clearly heard within the boat. The air grew more foul the longer the hunt continued. Men perspired and grew white-faced as the "pings" quickened with proximity; they felt the kick of exploding depth-charges and watched with horror as green seawater poured in through buckled plates.

Though the coming of corvettes helped the escort problem, more and more were needed. The year 1940 ended heavily in Germany's favour. But despite serious losses the Allies that year gained something that Hitler could never hope to have — the help of the United States.

93. A U-boat, brought to the surface by depth charges, slides under.

The Ship That Won the War

Roosevelt acts

American help for the Allies came about through the accident of history that brought Franklin Roosevelt and Winston Churchill together as leaders of their countries in the Second World War. They had met only once, in July 1918. Roosevelt, then Woodrow Wilson's Assistant Secretary of the Navy, had visited London and attended a dinner for the War Cabinet at which Churchill was present; neither, it is fair to say, made much impression on the other. On 5 September 1939, two days after Britain and France declared war on Germany, President Roosevelt proclaimed American neutrality. Yet only six days later he invited Churchill, member of the cabinet of a foreign belligerent nation, to enter into direct correspondence with him. It was an extraordinary thing to do. Churchill responded and, as First Lord of the Admiralty, began to provide Roosevelt with explanations of British naval policy and actions. In all these early messages he sought to gain Roosevelt's trust and build in him a sense of common purpose. He succeeded. Close to 2,000 messages passed between Churchill and Roosevelt during the war, an unprecedented exchange that, despite differences, led to personal friendship, a pooling of resources, a planning of common strategy and a meshing of military and diplomatic effort that was to be the meat of victory, and not only in Atlantic waters.

In 1939, as an Anglo-French staff report confirmed, both Britian and France would have to rely upon the United States for a large range of raw materials and manufactured goods in the event of war. The U.S. Neutrality Act of 1936, however, made it mandatory for the President to declare an arms embargo, forbidding the supply of arms to any belligerent state. Not only that. Loans were forbidden to countries that had not cleared their

First World War debts, and both Britain and France still owed the United States money from that war. Both had ordered armaments. If they were unable to collect them, or to finance future shipments, the outlook was bleak for a long war. In the first month of the war, Roosevelt obtained the co-operation of South America in keeping the Western Hemisphere neutral. The Declaration of Panama (2 October), proclaimed western Atlantic waters from the Canadian border to the tip of South America a neutral zone, forbidden to any belligerent. This was clearly aimed at Germany. The U.S. navy, with 80 destroyers, patrolled the zone, which extended seaward from 300 to as much as 1,000 miles. On 29 October 1939 the Senate — carefully primed by Roosevelt — approved amendments to the Neutrality Act that would allow Britain and France to draw on American industrial might; sanction by the House of Representatives followed one week later. The first round in the political battle of the Atlantic had been won, though arms could only be collected on a "cash and carry" basis.

Sure of Roosevelt's sympathy by the time he became Prime Minister on 10 May 1940, Churchill asked for the loan of "forty or fifty of your older destroyers," bluntly pointing out that "the voice and force of the United States may count for nothing if they are withheld too long." Though France was falling, Roosevelt felt the time not yet right for an approach to Congress — isolationist feeling was strong and a presidential election campaign in progress. The isolationists were fanned by Nazi undercover agents, among them wealthy Texas oil dealer William Rhodes Davis, through whom a million and a half dollars of Nazi money was funnelled in an effort to prevent Roosevelt's re-election. In association with John L. Lewis of the United Mineworkers, Davis tried to swing five

September 11, 1939.

My dear Churchill:-

It is because you and I occupied
similar positions in the World War that I
want you to know how glad I am that you are
back again in the Admiralty. Your problems
are, I realize, complicated by new factors
but the essential is not very different.
What I want you and the Prime Minister to
know is that I shall at all times welcome
it if you will keep me in touch personally
with anything you want me to know about.
You can always send sealed letters through
your pouch or my pouch.

I am glad you did the Marlboro
volumes before this thing started -- and I
much enjoyed reading them.

With my sincere regards,

Faithfully yours,

The Right Honorable
            Winston Churchill, P.C., C.H.,
                First Lord of the Admiralty,
                    London,
                        England.

94. The unsigned carbon copy of Roosevelt's request
that Churchill correspond directly with him.

Roosevelt Acts

million workers' votes against the President. William Stephenson, the discreet and influential Canadian who headed British Security Co-ordination in New York (Churchill code-named him "Intrepid" and used him as an intermediary between himself and Roosevelt) exposed such men, as well as pro-Nazi American business interests; and eventually Roosevelt froze all Axis funds.

96. The first six U.S. destroyers received by Canada berthed at Halifax in September 1940. Foreground, left to right, *St. Clair, Niagara, Annapolis*; rear, *Columbia, St. Francis, St. Croix*.

95. Sir William Stephenson ("Intrepid") receives the U.S. Medal for Merit, November 1946, from William J. Donovan, Director of the U.S. Office of Strategic Services — forerunner of the C.I.A. — "for timely and invaluable aid to the American war effort". He was the first non-American to be so decorated. Lady Stephenson is at the right.

As for the destroyers, broad agreement was reached in September and the "deal" consummated in detail following President Roosevelt's re-election to an unprecedented third term of office. Britain acquired not only 50 over-age destroyers — of which six (and later a seventh) were passed to Canada — but also five B-17 (Flying Fortress) bombers and 250,000 rifles with five million rounds of ammunition. In exchange, Britain granted long-term leases to the United States for the construction of American bases in various British possessions in the Western Hemisphere, including Newfoundland. The whole arrangement had come about very largely because of the trust and understanding that had already developed between the two men.

While this "deal" was in progress, urgent lists of arms, equipment and ammunition deemed essential to stiffen British defences against the German threat of invasion were pouring into the office of Arthur Purvis, head of the British Purchasing Mission in New York. Purvis, a Canadian, had close contacts with the American business world. By June, Purvis had engineered a formula whereby the U.S. could legitimately dispose of "surplus" armaments, and American arsenals were tapped for supplies

97. American supplies being loaded, at the port of New York, aboard freighters bound for Britain.

Roosevelt Acts

98. U.S. aircraft for Britain. Gunners man the guns that were installed to help protect such ships and their cargoes on the transatlantic route.

totalling $38 million. On 10 June, the day Mussolini declared war, the first shipment — 48 field guns, 15,000 machine guns, 12,000 rifles and 37 million rounds of ammunition — was on its way to Britain.

The day after Roosevelt had received Churchill's plea for destroyers, the President set in train a series of efforts that would transform the American armed forces — which consisted, at the time, of an army of only five divisions (weak in armour), an air force largely equipped with obsolete or obsolescent aircraft and a navy that was not yet equal to the Japanese. These preparations — which would, for example, make America the strongest airpower in the world — gave the United States a timely start in the all-out industrial struggle that was coming and undoubtedly shortened the war.

In mid-June Churchill cabled Roosevelt: ''The fate of the British fleet . . . would be decisive on

Roosevelt Acts

In 1942
America Will Build

60.000

WAR PLANES

In 1943
America Will Build

125.000

WAR PLANES

Franklin D Roosevelt

PUBLISHED BY THE UNITED STATES OF AMERICA

99.

100. U.S. and Canadian members (and their advisers) of the Permanent Joint Board on Defence (1942). O.M. Biggar, Canadian chairman, is sixth from the left (front row) with Mayor Fiorello La Guardia, the American chairman, at the extreme right. Brigadier Georges Vanier (wearing greatcoat) is at the centre.

the future of the United States because if it were joined to the fleets of Japan, France and Italy and the large resources of German industry, overwhelming sea power would be in Hitler's hands. . . . If we go down you may have a United States of Europe under the Nazi command far more numerous, far stronger, far better armed than the new [world]."

The New World included Canada, and on 17 August, at Roosevelt's invitation, Mackenzie King met the President in his private railway car on a siding near the station of Ogdensburg, New York. The Canada–United States Permanent Joint Board on Defence resulted, through which Canada and the United States studied the problems of the defence of this continent even though the United States and Germany were not yet at war. The studies related to sea, land and air problems — including manpower and material. It prepared the measures through which the continued existence of the two countries would be ensured. It was, in fact, an alliance, no matter how informal, and the use of the word "permanent" in the title left no doubt that the partnership would continue in the post-war years (as it does today). An invasion could not be ruled out if Britain should be defeated and her fleet fall into German hands.

That same summer the National Resources Mobilization Act, introduced by Mackenzie King, received assent in Canada. This authorized compulsory military service but, honouring the pledge that the government had made at the outbreak of the war, limited it to home defence. Thousands of "NRMA men" were to be enrolled.

In December Churchill gained another victory. That month Roosevelt abolished "cash and carry" — the basis of trade whereby Britain paid for imports from the United States in dollars (that were fast becoming exhausted) and carried much-needed food and armaments in her own ships from United States ports — substituted "lend-lease" for it.* Roosevelt explained it to his people in a simple way. Suppose your neighbour's house was on fire, he said; you would lend him a hose-pipe to put it out and your neighbour would naturally return the hose-pipe afterwards. It was the same with the implements of war and America must be the great arsenal of democracy.

101. Allied warships anchored at Hvalfjordur Harbour, Iceland, which was developed by the British and taken over by the Americans in 1941.

In 1941 he went further by ordering the protection by the U.S. navy of lend-lease supplies; it was done gradually to overcome the opposition of isolationists, who were very strong, and of Congress. In July 1941, U.S. marines replaced the British garrison in Iceland (which included one Canadian brigade), a move "cordially welcomed" by Churchill, for it freed a division for the Middle

*In answer to this appeal by Churchill on 7 December 1940: "The moment approaches when we shall no longer be able to pay cash for shipping and other supplies. While we will do our utmost and shrink from no proper sacrifice to make payments . . . I believe that you will agree that it would be wrong in principle and mutually disadvantageous in effect if, at the height of the struggle, Great Britain were to be divested of all saleable assets so that after victory was won with our blood, civilisation saved, and time gained for the United States to be fully armed against all eventualities, we should stand stripped to the bone."

Roosevelt Acts

102. Roosevelt and Churchill meet off Argentia, Newfoundland where they drew up the Atlantic Charter in August 1941.

East and it helped build up the Canadian formations in Britain. The U.S. navy began to escort convoys between the United States and Iceland, as was logical. But not only were American and Icelandic ships offered protection; so were ships of any nationality that cared to join. Thus, though in theory only safeguarding its own lines of communications, in practice the United States was escorting British merchantmen in western North Atlantic waters and U.S. warships — though not themselves attacking — were notifying British units of the whereabouts of U-boats.

Churchill and Roosevelt met for the first time during the Second World War aboard their respective warships *Prince of Wales* and *Augusta* at Placentia Bay, Newfoundland, in August 1941. The "Atlantic Charter" resulted, a declaration of joint Anglo-American aims that included "the right of all people to choose the form of government under which they will live" and looked to a peace in which "all the men in all the lands may live out their lives in freedom from fear and want." Roosevelt left the meeting well pleased. Churchill, who had not budged Roosevelt from his stand of "all aid short of war," was nevertheless "sure I have established warm and deep personal relations with our great friend," and in that lay the greatest significance of the conference. There were material benefits for Britain. In mid-September Roosevelt advised Churchill that he had established a production schedule for tanks that would aim at 1,400 a month in May 1942, rising to a maximum monthly figure of 3,000 at full capacity. He had studied production plans and looked at the suggested monthly figure; then he had placed a cigarette in his long holder, lit it, and said calmly: "Double it!"

Bases for ships and aircraft had been established in Newfoundland as well as in Iceland early in 1941. Those in Newfoundland became Canada's responsibility and in June all Canadian destroyers were concentrated there with the first seven Canadian-built corvettes. In October, however, the Canadian naval forces were put under American naval supervision (a tactful move, perhaps, in view of Roosevelt's increasing commitment), even though America was still neutral; the move did not please Canada. Nevertheless, Canadians initiated Americans into the intricacies of convoy warfare, and co-operation and relationships between the personnel of both navies proved excellent.

Earlier, on 4 September, a German U-boat fired two torpedoes at the U.S. destroyer *Greer some*

200 miles southwest of Iceland. *Greer* had been following the submarine for three hours, and broadcasting its location, before the U-boat suddenly attacked. The torpedoes missed, and though Roosevelt had to be cautious (as late as October 1941, public opinion pools showed that between 75 and 80 per cent of the American people were strongly opposed to direct intervention in the war), he took the opportunity of issuing orders to the Atlantic fleet on 13 September whereby U.S. warships could henceforth escort convoys of any nationality and destroy any German or Italian naval or air forces that they might encounter. Hitler had his hands full in Russia; despite the provocation, he did not retaliate by declaring war. A month later, however, the destroyers USS *Kearny* and USS *Reuben James* were torpedoed with the loss of 126 lives. It is hard to escape the conclusion that, though Pearl Harbor was weeks away, in the cold waters of the North Atlantic the United States was already at war.

103. USS *Kearny* after having been torpedoed by a U-boat in October 1941. Eleven men were killed and 24 wounded. The destroyer managed to reach Iceland under her own power.

Roosevelt Acts

1941
The balance sheet

104. A westbound convoy steams towards the setting sun.

On balance, 1941 was a little brighter than the previous year despite the German U-boat building programme that was to see the fleet grow to 233 boats at the year's end. The British lost 1,299 ships (4,328,558 tons worldwide, more than three million in the North Atlantic) for 35 U-boats destroyed; but new construction had added nearly two million tons (815,000 from the U.S.A.). Thus the net tonnage loss had decreased from three million in 1940 to 2,414,000 in 1941, but the battle was still being lost.

Both the Royal Navy and the Royal Canadian Navy had built up rapidly in anti-submarine escort vessels — destroyers, including the old American destroyers, as escort leaders and the newly-produced corvettes. Canada gradually extended her cover eastwards; Britain towards the west. In May 1941 the two navies met to provide an eastbound convoy with continuous protection across the North Atlantic for the first time, and in July the first westbound convoy received the same protection. With increasing American commitment, U.S. ships took over from Canadian escorts at a Western Ocean Meeting Point south of

105. The cold, grey seas in Arctic waters.

Newfoundland and escorted them to a Mid-Ocean Meeting Point off Iceland where British ships took over. The same practice applied to returning convoys. However, the "black pit" (as the Germans called it), the area that could not be patrolled by air from either Britain, Iceland or Newfoundland, remained devoid of aircraft cover and a killing-ground for Allied ships.

Churchill's offer of aid to Russia as soon as Hitler invaded that country in June 1941 brought another responsibility — that of opening up a new convoy route, mainly by diverting ships carrying American-made munitions bound for Britain in Icelandic waters and sending them around the North Cape of Norway to Murmansk. This was the most

hazardous route of all, and not only because of weather; it was to come within reach of German aircraft in northern Norway and of German surface ships in the northern Norwegian fjords as well as submarines. Early convoys to North Russia got through safely but later ones were badly mauled.

By the end of 1941 Germany had discontinued attacks by surface warhsips. These ships had been highly effective, especially against unescorted merchantmen; they also tied up ships of the Royal Navy that could have been better used elsewhere. Stephen Roskill, official historian of British naval operations, states that between 23 January and 22 March 1941 *Scharnhorst* and *Gneisenau* "not only sank or captured 22 ships . . . but also, for a time, completely dislocated our convoy cycles, with serious consequences to our vital imports. Their depredations forced the wide dispersal of our already strained naval resources.'' Losses in the Atlantic from all causes in the month of March totalled 529,706 tons (out of which 243,020 were lost to U-boats, 139,906 to surface warships and raiders), the highest monthly loss in the war so far and a rate of loss that Britain could not long survive. Raeder's major plan for 1941 was to bring together as a raiding squadron his battleship *Bismarck*, newly completed, the new heavy cruiser *Prinz Eugen* (both in the Baltic) and *Scharnhorst* and *Gneisenau* from the French port of Brest. This would be a combination that could tackle any convoy, no matter how strongly escorted, for *Bismarck* — with eight 15-inch guns, thick armour plate, a speed of 30 knots and six aircraft — was the most powerful vessel afloat. All this, Raeder hoped, would have a decisive effect on the Atlantic struggle. *Scharnhorst* and *Gneisenau*, however, could not join the squadron; the former had

developed engine trouble and the latter had been severely damaged in an RAF raid on Brest by a torpedo bomber piloted by Flying Officer Kenneth Campbell. Campbell's aircraft was shot to pieces seconds after scoring a hit on *Gneisenau*'s stern that crippled the warship for six months.* The squadron commander, Admiral Gunther Lûtjens, counselled delay until *Tirpitz* (*Bismark*'s sister-ship, then completing) would be available, but Raeder, with tankers and supply ships on the way to remote rendezvous points, would not wait and on 18 May the two ships left the Baltic to break out into the Atlantic. They were detected by a British reconnaissance aircraft, and the Home Fleet, as well as Force ''H'' at Gibraltar, steamed north to intercept.

The Germans scored the first victory when *Bismarck* sank HMS *Hood* near the Denmark Strait on 24 May. There were only three survivors; 95 officers and 1,320 men were lost. *Bismarck*, down by the bows from a hit from HMS *Prince of*

106. The destination, Murmansk (as seen through the side of an Allied ship).

*Campbell's navigator was Sergeant James Scott, a Canadian from Toronto, who was killed with him.

107. The British battle-cruiser, HMS *Hood,* photographed on the day she was sunk (24 May 1941).

Wales (battleship), slipped away from her British pursuers and on the morning of the 25th had broken contact; had Admiral Lütjens remained silent he might have escaped, but instead he transmitted a long radio message to Germany giving an account of his action with *Hood* at a time when every direction-finding station on both sides of the Atlantic was keeping watch on *Bismarck*'s frequency. Direction-finding, based on General McNaughton's* pre-war Canadian invention of the cathode-ray direction finder, had become extremely useful in the Atlantic war. With sets installed, for example, in the south of England, the north of Scotland and at various locations on Canada's Atlantic seabord, a number of different bearings would result and the intersection of those would accurately position *Bismarck*. It was known that the transmission came from *Bismarck*; the radio of each particular ship and/or operator had characteristics that were easily identified when the display on the cathode tube was photographed and compared with the "radio fingerprints" of German ships. Force

*McNaughton, from 1939, commanded the Canadian troops in Britain.

"H" and HMS *Rodney* were at once alerted in *Bismarck*'s direction, as was the Home Fleet some time later. Three Canadian destroyers, supporting the heavy ships, took part in the hunt: *Saguenay, Assiniboine,* and *Columbia* (one of the old, "four-stacker", ex-American destroyers). Carrier-borne aircraft located and crippled the German vessel. On the morning of 27 May *Bismarck*, pounded by gunfire into a ragged hulk, was sent to the bottom by torpedoes. Only 110 survived; more than 2,000 officers and men were lost.

Prinz Eugen reached Brest, but Hitler, with the loss of *Bismarck*, abandoned surface raids in the open Atlantic. The name of the pocket battleship *Deutschland* (Germany) had in fact already been changed to *Lützow*, for Hitler, who lived in constant dread of the possible fate of major ships, could not tolerate the thought of the sinking of one named *Deutschland*.

In 1942, however, *Prinz Eugen, Scharnhorst* and *Gneisenau,* then repaired, left Brest, which was under constant attack by the RAF, and succeeded in

109. *Scharnhorst, Gneisenau* and *Prinz Eugen* (screened by smaller ships) off Dunkirk during their daring "Channel dash".

108. *Bismarck*, photographed on 24 May 1941, is down
by the bows after a hit from HMS *Prince of Wales*.

110 & 111 Italian submarines, both lost in the Mediterranean towards the end of 1940.

Britain, when Britain herself turned to the bombing of Germany, it was certain (despite wishful thinking) that war at long-range, conducted by bombers, had shaken the morale of neither country. There was no practicable way for Germany to come to grips with Britain by land, for the Channel daunted the Germans; Britain was far too weak to invade the Continent. It was deadlock. Hitler made up his mind to conquer Russia and in May 1941, with plans in preparation, discontinued his bomber offensive against Britain.

The main British base in the Middle East was Egypt, threatened by Italian forces in Libya; and this was a theatre in which the British could fight. In August 1940, when the Battle of Britain was at its height, Churchill had ordered one-third of existing tank strength to Egypt. Italian troops in North and East Africa (Libya, Abyssinia and Eritrea) numbered some 400,000; to oppose them General Sir Archibald Wavell, the British commander, had some 80,000 troops, most of them in Egypt and Palestine. In December 1940 the British, with Australians and New Zealanders, struck at Sidi Barrani and, though grossly outnumbered, had by nightfall taken so many prisoners that it was impossible to make an early count. In the words of a Coldstream Guards officer there were about "five acres of officers and a hundred acres of other ranks". By the first week of February 1941 all Libya, including the ports of Tobruk and Benghazi, had been wrested from the Italians. In East Africa British troops advancing from the Sudan, with South African troops moving north from Kenya, invaded Abyssinia and Eritrea. The Italians were defeated; Emperor Haile Selassie of Abyssinia returned to his capital. With this the Red Sea was cleared and there was no longer any

making a dash up the English Channel to the relative safety of the German North Sea ports. Through audacity, radar jamming and strong fighter protection, the ships ran the gauntlet of aircraft, guns and mines — with damage, but they got through. Both *Scharnhorst* and *Gneisenau* struck mines; repairs kept the former out of action for several months. *Gneisenau* docked at Brunsbüttel for minor repairs and there RAF Bomber Command damaged her so severely that she took no further part in the war. With *Tirpitz* in northern Norway, however, Hitler had ships that would always pose a threat to the convoys passing around the North Cape to Russia; but no more would they sink vessels in the North Atlantic. That would be left to Doenitz and his U-boats.

Once again, as in 1940 with Hitler's conquest of northern and western Europe, events on land in 1941 affected those by sea. After the Battle of

112. British warships, seen here off Gibraltar, reinforce the Mediterranean.

113. German paratroops landing near Suda Bay, Crete, 20 May 1941.

danger in delivering supplies by sea to Suez. And Admiral Cunningham — on 11 November 1940 — had smashed the Italian fleet, stronger than the British in the Mediterranean, in the harbour of Taranto with aircraft from the carrier *Illustrious*. In all half the Italian battle fleet was put out of action, so that the British recovered command of the eastern Mediterranean. That victory was consolidated in April 1941 when, off Cape Matapan, the British sank three Italian cruisers and two destroyers.

In October 1940 Mussolini, frustrated by Marshal Graziani's reluctance to march on Egypt, had invaded Greece from the Albanian border without consulting Hitler. Six weeks later the Italians were not fighting in Greece; they had been driven back into Albania and were in serious trouble. So much so that on 4 December Mussolini received a report from Albania that the military situation was beyond redemption.

Mussolini, swallowing his pride, appealed to Hitler for help against the Greeks. And Hitler responded. Invited by Roumanian dictator Ion Antescu, he had occupied Roumania at the end of October 1940; Roumania was to be his major source of oil. Both that country and Hungary joined Germany in November. Now Hitler promised

Greek territory to Bulgaria, and on 1 March 1941 Bulgaria joined the Axis. On the following day the German Twelfth Army moved to the north of the Greek frontier. In March, with invasion imminent, 62,000 British, Australian, New Zealand and Polish troops left North Africa for Greece by treaty and at Greek invitation. Thus Wavell, who had expected to drive the Italians out of North Africa — there was nothing to stop him — was forced to dissipate his strength.

Hitler needed to cross Yugoslavia, as well as Bulgaria, to make a speedy end of Greece. Representatives of the regent, Prince Paul, succumbed to Hitler's bullying in Vienna and signed a treaty with him on 24 March. But the Yugoslavs, incensed, overthrew the regent, proclaimed the young King Peter ruler and scrapped the treaty. The enraged Hitler turned to the destruction of Yugoslavia — including the massive bombing of Belgrade — which he accomplished in ten days; and the turn of Greece had come.

The Germans entered Athens on 27 April. The British managed to evacuate 60,000 troops (50,000 Commonwealth and Poles, and 10,000 Greeks). Many of them went to Crete, which the Germans captured by paratroops; but they were so mauled that never again did Hitler attempt the conquest of any place by purely airborne forces. Thus Malta, important to our later story, survived.

The Balkan campaign, so costly for the Allies, had however one effect that cannot be overlooked. It caused Hitler to postpone his invasion of the Soviet Union from 15 May to 22 June — only a few weeks, but every day of good campaigning weather was to prove crucial in the fall of 1941, when the onset of winter deprived Hitler of the victory he had expected to win in eight weeks. Some have argued that mid-May, because of the late thaw in 1941, was too early for the use of armour in any case, and that the date would have had to have been set back even without the Balkan distraction. But soft ground conditions did not impose a *five-week* postponement; the German need to recover armour from the Balkans did.

Two circumstances are of immediate concern to us. The first is that Germany sent troops to North Africa to bail out Mussolini there. German aircraft, based in Sicily, assured Axis control of the central Mediterranean and threatened Malta, Britain's "indestructible aircraft carrier", which constantly

interfered with Axis supplies to North Africa and, still in British hands, was to be a major factor in the later conquest of North Africa and the freeing of the Mediterranean to Allied shipping. Secondly, with Germany's invasion of Russia, Churchill offered an immediate alliance to Stalin (he admitted that he would have made an alliance with the devil to defeat Hitler), which meant supplying Russia with war materials around the Arctic route to the North Russian ports of Archangel and Murmansk. This Churchill did by renouncing war material from the United States in favour of Russia, for which he got no thanks, and which was expensive in that it slowed the build-up of British forces. That was the dawn of the Arctic convoys. But before we deal with them, we must turn to the North Atlantic.

The submarines started badly in 1941. For one thing, January and February in the North Atlantic were two of the worst months on record. One U-boat commander has described the winds that howled at gale force from, it seemed, every quarter, driving the rain in sheets across towering seas that

114. A British convoy fights through to Malta.

1941

115 & 116. Rough seas also affected U-boat operations.

were only a few degrees above zero. The watch had to be lashed to the rail to save him from being washed overboard by the force of the breaking waves. Tons of green seawater swept over the icy, glistening metal of the boat, choking the mouth and nostrils of the man on watch, blinding his eyes and soaking him to the skin. Binoculars, held in stiff, frozen hands, were almost useless. U-boat operations were sharply curtailed; Allied shipping losses dropped, though they would mount again with better weather.

In the crowded little corvettes it was almost as bad, though the men were not quite so close to the sea. Given the corvettes' pitching and rolling, it was always necessary to hang onto something. Snatching sleep behind bulkheads beaded with moisture, the men wedged themselves into hammocks with sodden blankets.

March brought calmer seas. The U-boat packs rallied and losses to merchantmen climbed sharply. But it was not completely one-sided, for in March alone Germany lost Gunther Prien, Joachim Schepke (both sunk with their boats) and Otto Kretschmer (who survived — captured — after the

117. Prien is congratulated by Admiral Saalwächter (Navy Group West) after his exploit at Scapa Flow. A popular hero in Germany, the Nazis kept Prien's death a secret for several months knowing it would affect morale.

sinking of his boat), three of the top-scoring U-boat aces. It was Prien who had penetrated Scapa Flow to sink the *Royal Oak*; Kretschmer was the leading ace, with 266,629 tons of shipping to his credit.

There were reasons for these and later successes that year. Starting in 1941 escort groups, which had trained together at the Hebrides base at Tobermory, were kept together for convoy duty. Previously there had hardly been any co-ordination between escort ships (there were all too few of them, as we have seen) haphazardly collected as they became available; and this was very apparent when convoys were assailed by U-boats. In February control became more intimate when the Commander-in-Chief Western Approaches moved from Plymouth to Liverpool, where he was in close touch with Atlantic shipping. An analysis of sinkings led to an increase in the size of convoys. It was concluded that the number of ships lost in any convoy was related to the number of attacking U-boats and to the number of escorting ships — not to the number of ships in the convoy. The larger the convoy, it seemed clear, the more ships got through; it is a fact of geometry that two small convoys have a greater perimeter to be defended than a single convoy twice the size. Convoys were doubled, and, as more escorts were becoming available, more were provided.

Radar began to be provided for use in escorts in the spring of 1941. Surfaced U-boats could now be "seen" at night, and it is significant that *U-100*

118. A depth-charged U-boat sinks.

(Schepke) was located (and later sunk) on a pitch-black night in March at a range of well over a mile by the British destroyer *Vanoc*, one of the first escorts to be equipped with radar. Another electronic device, less complicated than radar, also came into use. This was a high frequency direction finder (Huff-Duff), which worked on the same principle as the shore-based radio direction finders that had picked up *Bismarck*'s transmission and established the position of the ship through the intersection of two or more bearings on the transmitted signal. Doenitz, we have noted, relied on radio transmissions from a "spotting" U-boat to concentrate the other members of the pack on convoys; messages exchanged between boats and headquarters usually enabled the British Admiralty to fix the submarines' positions. The information, when passed on, was rarely timely enough for escorts to act on it, however; only when shipborne Huff-Duff appeared — enabling two ships of an escort to get their own fix on a U-boat (with greater accuracy than shore stations hundreds of miles away) — could the escorts act at once and close in together for the kill.

Communications between ships also improved. These had depended on visual signals by day and coded radio messages at night — both slow, and the latter impracticable under battle conditions when speed was vital. The solution was found in very high frequency radio telephones that enabled one ship to talk directly to neighbouring ships during an attack. The system was eventually expanded to

aircraft to facilitate teamwork between air and surface units.

To illuminate U-boats surfaced at night, there had always been star-shell; but flashes from the guns projecting it temporarily blinded the lookouts at the very moment when the bursting shell provided light over the dark surface of the sea. "Snowflake" — rockets that soared up with minimal flash — solved the problem and was, in any case, brighter than star-shell. Here again, as with developing protective measures against the magnetic mine, Charles Goodeve was instrumental in the development of the new weapon. Snowflake was a mixed blessing, however, and had to be used with care, for it starkly revealed to lurking U-boats both the ship that fired it and neighbouring merchantmen. But used in conjunction with radar — with guns and depth charges ready — it did more good than harm.

The importance of air cover, recognized in the First World War, had not been forgotten, but Coastal Command was the "Cinderella" of the RAF at the outbreak of war, having no more the 170 seaplanes and land-based aircraft, most of them obsolete and of limited range. New aircraft, of necessity, were built for Fighter Command to use in the crucial air battles over Britain and for Bomber Command to take the war to Germany in the months thereafter. At the beginning of 1941 Coastal Command had acquired no more than 50 extra aircraft. Like destroyers in the early days, even these were misemployed in wide "search and patrol" sweeps instead of sticking close to convoys. Even if a U-boat happened to be spotted, the small bombs carried had to be aimed "by guess and by God" — there were no bombsights; strikes were rarely effective. Modified depth charges, fitted with fins, were introduced, and these were far more lethal.

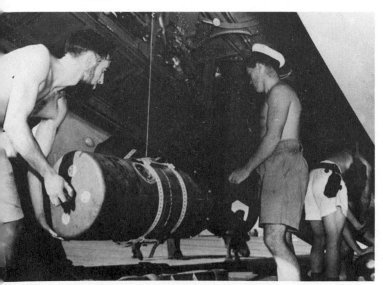

119. An airborne depth charge being loaded.

120. A Catalina flying-boat of Coastal Command patrols Atlantic waters.

In 1941, Coastal Command received a boost: 30 American PBY "Catalina" flying boats (the amphibian version was known as the "Canso" aircraft to Canadians). These had roughly 24 hours' endurance at cruising speed, which vastly improved the coverage of convoys. Together with a squadron of Lockheed Hudsons plus long-range fighters flying out of Iceland, they reduced the black pit by 400 miles. In the summer merchant ships equipped with catapults and fighter aircraft began to operate in the pit itself. In August a Hurricane from a CAM-ship (Catapult Aircraft Merchantman) scored the first victory when it shot down a Condor 400 miles from land. There were snags; the fighter could not be recovered. It had to find an airstrip or ditch close to a ship for the pilot to be picked up. Small escort carriers, which could recover aircraft, were to succeed CAM-ships; Canada would receive two new carriers (built in American shipyards) from the Royal Navy in 1944, and these she operated for the rest of the war.

Airborne radar (ASV — air to surface vessel) increased the effectiveness of aircraft as anti-submarine weapons, though contact was lost when the aircraft closed the target — a great disadvantage at night. This was solved by fitting a powerful "Leigh" searchlight to bridge the radar gap; it came into use in August 1941. Radar enabled an aircraft to spot a possible target at long range, cut its engines and swoop in silently to attack, flooding

121. A CAM-ship with a Hurricane on its launching ramp.

123. Cleaning the "Leigh" light of a Liberator. The brainchild of Squadron Leader H. de V. Leigh, RAF, the searchlight helped Coastal Command aircraft to strike surfaced U-boats at night.

her captain, Commander J.D. ("Chummy") Prentice*, an ex-Royal Navy officer who had retired to his ranch in British Columbia in 1934, attacked. Six depth charges dropped over the target ruptured the battery room; the submarine filled with chlorine gas and was forced to surface. *Moose Jaw* rammed, but it was a glancing blow. Prentice sent a boarding party to what was now seen to be *U-501*, when it was found that the seacocks had been opened; Stoker William Brown, who tried to close them, went down with the submarine, the first to be sunk by Canadian ships.

A U-boat torpedoed *Levis*, part of the escort for SC-44, also in Greenland waters, killing 18 seamen as they slept in their hammocks and wounding two. Though her port side was ripped open, the ship settled slowly. HMCS *Mayflower* (corvette), coming up in the dark, managed to get a towline across to the crippled vessel, which remained afloat for more than four hours before she lurched over and sank. Altogether *Mayflower* and HMCS *Agassiz* (another corvette) took off 40 survivors. *Windflower* was lost on a cold December morning when a freighter sheared off her stern in fog. The

124. Commander J.D. ("Chummy") Prentice, RCN. He received the DSO, when commanding HMCS *Chambly*, for his role in sinking *U-501*.

the target with a cold white glare when it was too late for the U-boat to escape.

September 1941 was a bad month for Canada. Towards the middle of September Convoy SC-42 of 64 ships escorted by the destroyer *Skeena* and corvettes *Alberni*, *Kenogami* and *Orillia* — joined later by two more corvettes, *Chambly* and *Moose Jaw* — lost 15 merchant ships, though *Chambly* and *Moose Jaw* sank a U-boat; on the 19th HMCS *Levis* (corvette) was sunk. Another corvette, *Windflower*, was lost through collision in December.

A wolf pack struck Convoy SC-42 between Greenland and Iceland at dusk on 9 September, sinking 10 merchant ships over the next 24 hours. The nights were milk-white, lit by the moon; icebergs, drifting south, studded the sea. On the night of the 10th *Chambly* and *Moose Jaw*, operating ahead of Convoy SC-42, swept back towards it. *Chambly* obtained an asdic contact and

122. The Hurricane is catapulted from the ramp; 12 cordite rockets were used to launch the fighter.

*James Douglas Prentice was a Canadian, brought up in British Columbia. He joined the RN as a career officer, was "axed" by the "Geddes axe," came home and joined the RCN at the outbreak of war.

125. The Italian submarine *Scire* carried the "two-man torpedoes" that sank British warships in Alexandria harbour.

ship blew sky high when her boilers burst, and 23 men died. It was unfortunate that HMS *Nasturtium*, a British corvette, mistook the explosion for a torpedoing and moved off through the Grand Banks' fog to investigate. She did, however, return in time to rescue, with the freighter, 47 of *Windflower*'s company, three of whom died later.

126. The torpedo, or midget submarine — ridden by frogmen — was 22 feet long and had a detachable warhead.

Despite the more-effective counter-measures that were coming in, it was perhaps fortunate for the Allies that on 22 November Hitler, who was aware that Rommel's campaign in North Africa depended on seaborne supplies, which were being cut off by the British Mediterranean Fleet, ordered the transfer of part of Doenitz's U-boat fleet from the Atlantic to the Mediterranean. There U-boats sank HMS *Ark Royal* (carrier) and HMS *Barham* (battleship), while six Italian frogmen, riding what were virtually two-man torpedoes, severely damaged two more battleships (HMS *Valiant* and HMS *Queen Elizabeth*) in the harbour of Alexandria. But sinkings in the North Atlantic, the most vital theatre, fell well below the October figures. Instead the waters off Gibraltar became highly dangerous for Allied shipping. Happily Gibraltar was not in German hands. In May 1941, it had seemed likely that Hitler would move against this British base, or make it untenable from either Spanish soil or Vichy French territory in North Africa. Should that happen, Churchill planned to seize the Spanish Canary Islands, and McNaughton's Canadian troops in Britain were alerted for the task. Franco, however, despite Hitler's mixed blandishments and threats, refused to be drawn, and without the right of free passage for German troops through Spain (with the invasion of Russia pending) Hitler did not move and the expedition against the Canaries became unnecessary. Britain's commitments in the Mediterranean and the Middle East, however, had

1941

increased. Pétain's government, in talks held early in May, permitted the Germans to use airfields in Syria (Vichy territory) from which the Suez Canal and oil refineries in Iraq and Persia (Iran) could be bombed. Britain moved first. Commonwealth (British, Indian and Australian) and Free French forces entered Syria on 8 June, overcoming the defending Vichy French army, which surrendered on 12 July. This was an added safeguard for vital oil supplies that were pumped across the Syrian Desert to the eastern Mediterranean shore from the oilfields of Iraq. As Churchill wryly pointed out to Roosevelt, "the fact that a government is a prisoner of war of another power does not justify such a prisoner in serving its conqueror in operations against its former ally". Then, in August, with the Germans well inside Russia and heading for the Caucasus, British and Russian forces occupied Iran. There were two main reasons for this: to open an "aid to Russia route" from the Persian Gulf overland to the Caspian Sea — less hazardous than the sea route to North Russia; and to safeguard the Iranian oil on which much of Britain's war effort depended.

In December, however, off Gibraltar, a 32-ship convoy, well escorted by ships that were equipped with radar and snowflake — and that were used to working together — exacted a toll of five U-boats for only two merchantmen lost in a running battle that lasted for a week. The last straw for Doenitz was the appearance of a four-engine Liberator bomber (the U.S. B-24), one of the first to be flown by Coastal Command, which had flown 800 miles from Britain to cover the convoy. Its depth charges forced one damaged U-boat to surface and scuttle itself. Given the port-to-port air cover that the Allies could now provide, Doenitz ordered the U-boats to cease their attacks.

It was an augury for the future, but more than a year would elapse before the submarine could be really countered.

127. A convoy runs the gauntlet off Gibraltar. An enemy bomb had narrowly missed a ship.

1942
Another desperate year

129. Hitler and his generals ponder strategy. Brauchitsch is on Hitler's right.

When 1942 opened the United States was formally at war on a global scale. Japan, at Pearl Harbor on 7 December 1941, had blasted America into the conflict. Britain declared war against Japan. Disappointingly for Churchill, Roosevelt had not automatically included Japan's allies — Germany and Italy — when he asked Congress to declare war against Japan; and should the United States become fully committed only in the Pacific theatre there was a real danger that Britain's position in the North Atlantic and in the Mediterranean would worsen.

Churchill need not have worried. Hitler solved the matter for him when, on December 11 — stating that "our patience has come to the breaking point" — he declared war on the United States. Mussolini followed suit. Faced with a new enemy, the Nazi strategists presented proposals to Hitler that would aim at crushing Britain before America could use her as a launching pad for an invasion of Europe. This would be accomplished in two steps: an all-out Mediterranean offensive in 1942; and an intensification of the Battle of the Atlantic, which would become the overriding campaign of the war. At first Hitler appeared to accept the proposals; but upon returning from Berlin to his command post on

128. Pearl Harbor under attack, 7 December 1941.

the Eastern Front he found his generals advocating a defensive campaign in Russia, which advice he stormily dismissed. He also dismissed von Brauchitsch, his Army Commander (taking command himself), as well as the "new" Western strategy, which he now termed "nonsense". Coupled with his declaration of war against the world's greatest industrial power, this was one of his gravest mistakes. It left him committed to offensive war in Russia that was to bleed his forces white; and through his decision with regard to the Atlantic he failed to disrupt the Anglo-American supply lines that would lead to the opening of other fronts — North Africa, Sicily and Italy, and finally that in Northwest Europe.

Roosevelt and Churchill were now allies in the world-wide struggle. For nearly three weeks in December 1941 and January 1942 the Prime Minister (who was accompanied by his military chiefs and his minister of war production, Canadian-born Lord Beaverbrook) conferred with Roosevelt in Washington. "The President . . . made the preliminary cocktails himself," Churchill recalled, "and I wheeled him in his chair . . . as a mark of respect." Much came out of this first Washington conference. The United States confirmed a strategy of "Germany first, then Japan", which was significant for Britain and a great concession in view of the animosity that had

130. Churchill and Roosevelt dine informally at the White House, January 1942.

been aroused in the United States by Japan's treacherous attack at Pearl Harbor. Churchill addressed Congress on 26 December, after which he was confident that he had won general support for his policy of defeating Hitler first. A "Combined Chiefs of Staff" was set up between the two countries, with headquarters in Washington, which was to do much to reconcile rival strategies. And a "United Nations Declaration" was signed by Roosevelt, Churchill and representatives of China and Russia that reaffirmed the principles set out in the Atlantic Charter and pledged each signatory to make no separate peace (and to use its full resources) until victory had been won. The "Grand Alliance" was born.

General George C. Marshall, Roosevelt's Army Chief of Staff (who has rightly been termed an "architect of victory"), supported the strategic war aims of the British, which were, roughly — to contain the Axis powers by sustaining the Russian front with supplies, and by increasing strength in

the Middle East with the goal of gaining possession of North Africa; and to transport air forces, troops, equipment and supplies to Britain so that U.S. bombers could join the offensive against Nazi war industries, while the ground forces would be available for a future invasion of the Continent. American troops would first relieve the British garrison in Northern Ireland. All this would depend on America's war production and her ability to transport men and supplies across the Atlantic. Production targets announced by Roosevelt in his New Year's message to the Congress were staggering: aircraft production to double in 1942, reaching 125,000 aircraft in 1943; tanks — again doubled, and rising to 75,000; 1942 ship construction to reach 8 million tons, rising in 1943 to 10 million.

Britain's output of shipping had increased; but with more limited resources it could not exceed 1¼ million tons a year. Canada turned to shipbuilding in a large way with the construction of "Fort" ships (named with the prefix *Fort* and a Canadian historical suffix) and "Park" ships (all named after Canadian parks). Starting in 1941, she constructed a total of 456 merchant ships, mainly of 10,000 tons, with a proportion of 4,700 tonners and some tankers. This amounted in all to just short of four million tons of shipping. The shipbuilding industry employed 57,000 people at the time of maximum production of merchant ships; a further 28,000 worked on the construction of naval ships. This was a tremendous effort for a country with Canada's population.

Canadian merchant ships, like the British, were riveted in the traditional manner. The Americans, on the other hand, starting with the *Patrick Henry* (launched in September 1941), had turned to prefabricated, welded ships. *Patrick Henry* took six months to build; thereafter production time for these "Liberty" ships of 10,000 tons shrank from month to month. In the spring of 1942 completion still took two months. In the fall the *Robert E. Peary* was finished in five days. By this time three ships were being launched daily. They were ugly, utilitarian, but they would float and carry cargo; and they were of enormous importance in the tonnage war, for if ships could be built faster than the U-boats could sink them, the war was won. In all, 2,700 Liberty ships were built during the war.

It is interesting to know what a 10,000-ton ship might carry at that stage of the war. Leslie Roberts, in *Canada's War at Sea*, describes a cargo: "on its decks two bomber aircraft with their wings in separate packing cases, enough aluminum in the hold to manufacture 640 fighter aircraft, 1,000 tons

131. A Canadian-built "Park" ship — the SS *Yoho Park*.

132. The launching of *Patrick Henry*, the first U.S. "Liberty" ship.

Launching SS Patrick
Fairfield, Md.
Sept. 27, 1941

134. A 10,000-ton merchant ship being loaded at Halifax. TNT goes in the hold; a tank is on the deck.

133. Roosevelt (back to camera) watches the launching of *Joseph N. Teal*, completed in 10 days. At this time (October 1942) three ships were launched every day.

of bombs, motor transport for a battalion of infantry, 2,150 tons of vital metals, lumber for 90 huts and 2,850 tons of food, sufficient to feed 225,000 people in the United Kingdom for a week''.

Another contribution, which so far has not been mentioned, was that of Ferry Command. In 1940 Lord Beaverbrook won Churchill's support for an ''Atlantic Ferry Organization'', manned by civilian pilots, to fly badly-needed bombers manufactured in North America direct to Britain. It was a daring concept at a time when only limited flying-boat crossings of the Atlantic had been attempted.

Sir Edward Beatty, president of Canadian Pacific Railways, took charge and by May 1941 deliveries had started. The aircraft generally flew from Montreal to a newly-built field at Gander, Newfoundland, thence to Northern Ireland or

Scotland. By August 315 aircraft had been delivered. That month ''Ferry Command, RAF'' replaced the civilian organization, and deliveries increased. By June 1943, for example, 2,240 aircraft were to have made the crossing safely. This saved shipping and was of great value in the strategic bombing of the Reich and the build-up for the invasion of Northwest Europe. It may seem ironic that, when the black pit was devoid of cover, bombers of Ferry Command were flying over it in a steady stream *en route* to Britain. But these bombers were ''stripped down'', their heaviest load being fuel. Armed with depth charges and a full crew, they would have had half the range that otherwise was possible.

America committed itself to furnish a quarter of Britain's food supply. This took the form of rich, concentrated foods such as cheese to save shipping space. Canada's aid was equally generous. Milk and eggs were dried, to concentrate them to the maximum, and the Ministry of Food in Britain

135. Both winter and summer, aircraft of Ferry Command spanned the Atlantic from Gander.

136. Ferry Command aircraft at Dorval (Montreal), ready for flight to Gander.

began to popularize the new foods through publicity. Since cattle took two years to rear, the Americans raised hogs for the British market, concentrating the meat and canning it as "Spam", rich in protein.

Though America's entry into the war would eventually be decisive, the immediate effect — in the Atlantic — was detrimental. Doenitz, whose U-boats had been hunted by U.S. escorts since the fall of 1941, had pressed for as much notice as possible of a state of war so that he could open it against U.S. shipping with, as he termed it, "a roll of drums". Though he started the year with 272 boats at his disposal, only about 90 were operational on any given day and of these 25 were in the Mediterranean at Hitler's order to prevent the supply of the British forces in the Western Desert; six were off the Gibraltar gateway; and four were stationed off Norway to cut the Allies' "aid to Russia" shipping route. That left 55 for Atlantic duty, of which an average of 13 were actively engaged each day for the first three months of 1942. These boats were of two types — the Type VII, standard for the North Atlantic, which had come into general service in 1941; and the Type IX, which had been specially built for operations farther afield. The VII had a low silhouette and a small conning tower, making it hard to spot. It was 220 feet long and of 769 tons displacement, and carried 14 torpedoes and a crew of 44. It had four torpedo

137. Food rationing was introduced in Canada during 1942. Meat and butter, as well as the three commodities shown, were rationed. This enabled surpluses to be sent to Britain.

138. The tempo of U-boat construction quickened as the war progressed. Krupp was a major manufacturer.

139. U-boats (Types VII and IX) at Trondheim, Norway.

140. Three Type VIIC U-boats at Wilhelmshaven (foreground) and a Type IXD (far left).

tubes forward and one at the stern as well as anti-aircraft armament. Its speed, surfaced, was 17 to 18 knots — slightly faster than a corvette. Type IX's were much larger, ranging from 1,000—1,600 tons, and were two knots faster. The largest boats of this type could cruise up to 23,000 miles (against some 8,000 miles for the VII and 13,000 for the smaller IXs) and thus could reach the Caribbean and

1942

141. A tanker goes down in smoke and flame off Cape Hatteras, North Carolina, 24 January 1942.

the South Atlantic. Type IXs carried 24 torpedoes (six tubes) and a crew of 57, and were well armed with anti-aircraft guns. Some IXs, with Doenitz's usual foresight, had been designed as supply submarines (''milch cows'') that carried spare torpedoes and oil for the other boats, which could thus extend their range and remain on patrol after their original complement of torpedoes had been expended. (The range of Allied escorts had been similarly extended by refuelling from tankers while at sea.) From May 1942 on, milch cows sustained the U-boat fleet.

The IXs, superior boats, had one disadvantage, which became apparent later when U-boats were to fear aircraft attack more than any other because of the speed with which it developed. The VII, when crash-diving, could be down in 25 seconds; whereas the IX, with its greater bulk, took 35 even in a calm sea. The U-boat needed to be 80 to 100 metres down to feel really safe, and that could rarely be achieved in time. Some captains preferred to stay up and fight with anti-aircraft guns; while they shot down some planes, the odds were with the aircraft.

Starting in January, Doenitz achieved staggering results with these boats — a second ''happy time'' for the U-boat captains comparable to the fall of 1940 when wolf-pack tactics had been first introduced. Directed to the eastern seaboard of the United States, from New England to Florida, the boats found easy pickings — no convoys; ships plying the regular shipping routes and using radio, as in peacetime; no aircraft cover; and ports and towns ablaze with lights from Maine to Miami's six-mile strip of neon. Ships, without protection and silhouetted against the coastal glow, were easy prey. Soon the roaring holocaust of blazing tankers,

bearing the lifeblood of the war, rivalled the bright displays ashore.

It is incomprehensible that Admiral Ernest J. King, commander-in-chief of the U.S. Navy, did not adopt the convoy system, tested in the crucible of war, that was still being followed by the few American escorts (well coached by Canadians and British) on the Iceland run. The British begged him to do so but, perhaps because of that, he set his face against it. True, he had his problems: most of his small warships were in the Pacific trying to oppose the Japanese, who were advancing through the Philippines and Southeast Asia. The bulk of those in the Atlantic were shepherding convoys that were now carrying troops as well as cargo, and the few that remained for the eastern seaboard he preferred to organize into hunter patrols — as the British had mistakenly done in the early months of the war. These offensive patrols, so dear to the heart of every naval officer who would otherwise be tied down to the humdrum work of convoy escort, did not kill a single U-boat until mid-April!

142. British and American leaders responsible for the naval war. Left to right: Admiral Ernest J. King, Churchill, A.V. Alexander (First Lord of the Admiralty), and Admiral Sir Dudley Pound (Chief of Naval Staff).

In March, contemplating colossal sinkings that amounted to some 80 ships, half of them tankers, the British Admiralty offered to send three dozen escorts and personnel to start a convoy system. By this time a coastal blackout, at least, had been enforced. King turned down the offer of men, but he did accept the ships. On 1 April he initiated a partial convoy system, covering the passage of ships in short moves of about 100 miles from port to port. By July this had become a full convoy system from the northern coast of South America all the way to Halifax, with ships joining or leaving a convoy at any port along the way. Together with air coverage, the system ended Doenitz's happy days; sinkings dropped from 23 in April to five in May and not a single ship was lost in July. HMCS *Oakville*, one of six Canadian corvettes lent to the U.S. Navy for Caribbean convoy duty, sank a U-boat in September. The corvette managed to get a small boarding party to the submarine, but the U-boat settled by the stern; an American destroyer picked up members of its crew. However, the U-boats had accounted for half a million tons of shipping off the American coast in the first six months of 1942.

U-boats had entered the St. Lawrence as soon as the ice was clear, sinking two ships on the night 11—12 May. They were to sink, in the River and the Gulf, 19 merchantmen and two warships — the armed yacht *Raccoon*, believed torpedoed by *U-165* and the corvette *Charlottetown*, sunk by *U-517*. (The frigate *Magog* followed much later, in October 1944).

Raccoon simply disappeared and the only trace ever found was the body of one man washed up on Anticosti Island. *Charlottetown*, with the minesweeper *Clayoquot*, had delivered a convoy to Rimouski on 11 September and was in the vicinity of Gaspé. Asdic conditions were very bad, as they usually were in the Gulf, where water temperatures vary at different depths, and neither ship detected the presence of a U-boat. Two torpedoes struck *Charlottetown* in quick succession and the ship sank in just three minutes. A depth charge went off, killing six of the men who had managed to get overboard and were struggling in the water, and injuring others. *Clayoquot*'s first duty was to hunt the submarine, which she did unsuccessfully before returning to pick up 55 survivors, among them many wounded.

These and other sinkings brought the war too close to Canada for Mackenzie King's liking. His answer was not to go after the submarines but to close the river, denying the port of Montreal to overseas shipping and the Allied cause. This slowed the export of badly-needed supplies, which had to be rerouted to the Atlantic ports, and cargoes shipped out of Canada fell by about a quarter. It was an inexpensive victory for the Nazis.

143. Hunter!

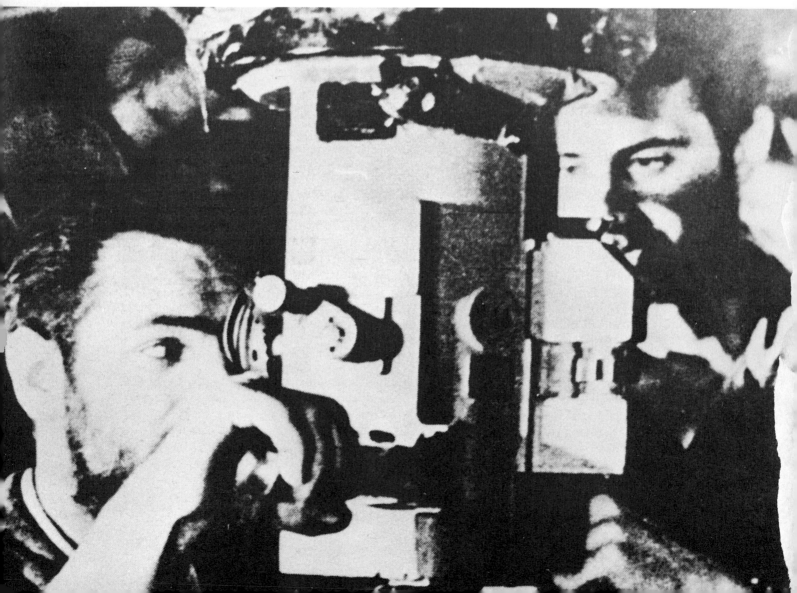

Thursday: Cloudy

THE OTTAWA EVENING JOURNAL

HOME EDITION

VOL. LVII.—No. 131.   OTTAWA, WEDNESDAY, MAY 13, 1942—TWENTY-FOUR PAGES.   PRICE THREE CENTS.

SHIP SUNK IN ST. LAWRENCE ON MERCY TRIP

Carried Survivors From Vessel Attacked Earlier

Believed Picked Up Elsewhere Than in St. Lawrence

A ST. LAWRENCE RIVER PORT, May 13.—(CP)—Nearly half of the more than four score survivors of a vessel torpedoed on Monday in the St. Lawrence river were reported to the Canadian Press today to have come from a vessel other than the one sunk by the first enemy submarine ever to invade the river waters.

Reports from various sources have indicated that either 87 or 88 survivors of the torpedo-sinking announced in Ottawa yesterday by Navy Minister Macdonald have reached land. Forty-one survivors are said to have been crew members of the vessel announced by the Navy Minister to have been sunk in the St. Lawrence. The others were aboard the same vessel but are said to have come originally from another ship.

No Details on Second.

It was impossible to obtain any information as to what had happened to the second vessel. A reliable source at one of the points along the St. Lawrence River would only offer the information that "some of the survivors were originally from a ship other than the one announced yesterday as sunk."

The possibility was seen that these survivors might have been picked up elsewhere than in the St. Lawrence.

A Canadian Press correspondent at a St. Lawrence river port said he had been informed that two men are missing from the torpedoing announced by the Navy Minister. This correspondent said the information that two men are missing had come from one of the survivors.

The survivor was reported to have said that the two men had been asleep in their quarters near the bow of the ship. It was believed they were injured by the first of two torpedoes which crashed into the vessel. The first torpedo struck the bow and the second, fired when the submarine surfaced, plunged into the midsection.

When the submarine surfaced, it was said to have shone its spotlight on the already-stricken vessel, then, with the vessel clearly outlined in the blaze of light, the second torpedo was sent crashing home.

Gunfire Heard.

Although it was not confirmed from survivors, residents along the river were said to have heard gunfire — either indicating that the submarine had fired shells at the ship or that the ship was fighting back. No report was available immediately as to how many shells, if any, were actually fired. Earlier, a light censorship of news from a nearby fishing village, where some of the survivors are resting, prevented confirmation of reports some lives had been lost.

(See Also Page 12.)

Claim Gort Hit By Bomb Splinter

LONDON, May 13.—(CP)—The Rome radio claimed today that a bomb splinter pierced the left arm of Lord Gort, new Governor and Commander-in-Chief of Malta, as he arrived at his post on the Mediterranean island last week.

(There has been no report from British sources of an injury to Lord Gort.

(He took the oath of office as Governor and Commander-in-Chief Sunday before a chief justice whose hand was bleeding from cuts sustained during a heavy Axis raid a short time before. Bombs fell throughout the ceremony and a near-hit at one time made the officials flatten themselves on the debris-strewn ground).

Thrown From Buggy And Drowned

BROOKS, Alta, May 13.—(CP)—Swept into the muddy waters of the Bow river, near here, from a buggy when his startled team bolted into the stream, George South, 56-year-old farmer, was drowned yesterday while his wife stood on the shore unable to help.

King's Stable Wins Rare Double

NEWMARKET, England, May 13.— (CP) — The King's stable completed a rare double at Newmarket today when a filly, Sun Chariot, won the 1,000 guineas stakes after the Royal colt Big Game took the 2,000 guineas classic yesterday.

Sun Chariot was the even-money favorite.

It was the first time since 1902 that one stable had won both events and the first time Royal entries ever won both. Sun Chariot, beaten once in seven starts, has poured more than $30,000 in the Royal coffers.

Jap Drive Now 80 Miles Inside China

British Troops Are Retreating Into India

LONDON, May 13.—(CP)—The reinforced Japanese are striking northeastward in China's Yunnan province toward Poashan, 100 miles by air from the Burma border and 180 miles at the Burma Road today, the Chinese reported today.

Despatches from Chungking said the Japanese were moving up from Lungling—80 miles by road inside China—in an apparent attempt to strike at Paoshan from the west in an encirclement manoeuvre.

New Advance Begins.

Only last night the Chinese announced that the Japanese were pushed back from Lungling, the main forces being hurled clear back to the border, but that a new advance had begun with the arrival of reinforcements to the invaders.

In Burma itself, a strong Chinese force was reported engaging Japanese units south of Myitkyina, northern terminus of the Rangoon railway.

Concluded on Page 12, Col. 5.

Japs Prepare New Thrust

MELBOURNE, May 13.—(BUP)—A Japanese invasion fleet is re-assembling at island bases northeast of Australia, awaiting heavy naval reinforcements for a new offensive thrust, despatches from Allied advanced bases indicated today.

Warships and transports were reported at these bases. The main striking force had been scattered by the American-Australian naval victory in the Coral Sea, but it was believed to be virtually intact, insofar as key units went. It was apparently only awaiting reinforcements to strike a new blow which many believed would give Australia and the United States and Allied forces their supreme test.

Activities of Japanese ships, reported by American and Australian reconnaissance planes, and of the Japanese air force based at Rabaul in the Bismarck Islands and Lae on the north New Guinea coast, indicated that enemy reinforcements were arriving steadily.

Elephants Dispute Right-of-Way Mosquitoes Raid Burma Evacuees

Reporter Tells of Difficult Trip Over World's Worst Road to India

Darrell Berrigan, British United Press correspondent who covered the Burma campaign, has arrived in Calcutta after a difficult trip over mountain roads.

By DARRELL BERRIGAN

CALCUTTA, May 13.—(Delayed)—(BUP)—Elephants disputed the right-of-way, tigers and chimpanzees roamed the wilds around us, but the only thing that really attacked us were the over-sized mosquitoes that swarmed as we drove from Shwebo to Kalewa, on the Chindwin river. Then snakes and mosquitoes attacked the British Imperial Forces we left behind in Burma who were storming north along the Irrawaddy river, we drove from Shwebo to Kalewa, on the Chindwin river. The mosquitoes were already was starting to attack us, and we headed for Calcutta in two American jeeps. We

could understand therefore why the hill tribes refused to work in the valleys and why the British medical stations were stocking up on quinine to fight mosquito-borne malaria.

Heavy Rains Start.

When we decided it was time to get out of Burma ahead of the Japanese who were storming north along the Irrawaddy river, we drove from Shwebo to Kalewa, on the Chindwin river. The monsoon season already was starting to break, roads were burning roads into quagmires and the rice fields into swamps.

Concluded on Page 12, Col. 7.

CANADA'S GAS RATIONS ARE REDUCED

Motorists Reduced to Category 'A'

Oil Controller Orders Drastic Cut

A general and drastic cut of gasoline rations has been ordered by Oil Controller G. R. Cottrelle.

Cracking down on the waste of gasoline burned in non-essential driving, the Oil Controller has directed reductions to Category "A" in the ration ratings of all but an excepted few motorists.

Ration Unit Affected.

Basic ration of Category "A" motorists has been 60 units or 300 gallons a year, each unit being worth five gallons. And there was every possibility, the Oil Controller has warned, of a reduction in the worth-in-gallons of the ration unit.

"Mr. Cottrelle has ordered re-examination of the ration rating of every motorist in Canada" an official of the Munitions and Supply Department told The Journal this morning.

"And every motorist is being reduced to Category 'A' unless he is engaged in work essential to the economy of a nation at war."

The reclassification of ration ratings would cut "thousands and thousands" of motorists all across Canada, he added.

The point of a motorist being engaged in "work essential to the economy of a nation at war," was one being decided by the regional oil control offices.

A check is being kept by the Oil Controller on the reclassification done by the regional offices.

Concluded on Page 12, Col. 2.

Invite 16 Nations To Parley Here

An enlargement of the Air Training Conference which has been called to meet in Ottawa May 18 to include representatives of as many as 16 nations, instead of the eight nations invited in the first instance, has been decided upon.

The Governments of South Africa, Poland, India, Southern Rhodesia, Czechoslovakia, Belgium, Yugoslavia, Greece, and Russia now have been invited to attend in addition to the United States, the United Kingdom, Australia, New Zealand, The Netherlands, Norway and China which were invited at first. Air Minister Power told the House of Commons yesterday Russia is the only one which has not yet indicated it will be represented.

Concluded on Page 12, Col. 8.

Happy Over Release From Italian Prison Camp

The joy of being home again shows clearly on the faces of these British soldiers who were exchanged for Italian prisoners at Smyrna, Turkey. Nine hundred and nineteen Italian wounded, sick and protected personnel were exchanged for 129 British soldiers, including South Africans, Indians, New Zealanders and Australians. Most of these men were taken prisoner in the western desert, and had been in Italian camps for six to eight months prior to their arrival in Alexandria.

Pope Appeals For Second Front That of Family

VATICAN CITY, May 13.—(Vatican broadcast recorded by BUP at New York)—Pope Pius called upon the rulers of nations today to rally for preservation of the family in peaceful existence and warned them that the future of the world will be on their consciences.

Speaking on the 25th anniversary of consecration as a bishop, he said that the "second front, the front of the family", is threatened by war, and warned of the terrible destruction which future operations can bring.

Urges Peace With Justice.

He said he did not intend to make a specific peace offer since it was not likely to be accepted under the present circumstances, but he urged the leaders of nations to conclude a peace based on justice even if this did not satisfy all of their ambitions.

"I made peace offers in the early stages of the war, but without positive results, and such offers may even cause grievances and dissatisfaction in some countries," the Pope said.

Concluded on Page 12, Col. 4.

80,000 YUGOSLAVS KILLED.

MOSCOW, May 13.—(AP)—The official Soviet news agency Tass reported today that 80,000 Yugoslavs had been killed in Baczska Province of Yugoslavia since the Hungarian occupation.

Gallant Exploit At Madagascar Port

LONDON, May 13.—(CP)—An official source said today that the fall of the Madagascar port of Antsirane was precipitated by the "extremely gallant exploit" of a British destroyer which slid through the narrow, mined entrance to Diego Suarez Bay under fire of French batteries and landed 50 marines. Antsirane surrendered May 5.

Major Price Safe.

Only one member of the Royal Rifles of Canada of Quebec, the other Canadian battalion, is listed. He is Major J. H. Price, of Quebec.

The Manitoba regiment group on the list, presumably all officers of the Grenadiers, numbers 25, of whom 17 are listed from Winnipeg, while another, Lieut. B. W. Queen-Hughes, also of Winnipeg, lists his next-of-kin as his wife, Subaltern Gloria Queen-Hughes, now serving with the Canadian Women's Army Corps at Halifax.

13 Nazi Troop Planes Downed Off North Africa

CAIRO, May 13.—(AP)—Thirteen Junkers 52's, the German troop-carrying planes, and two of their Messerschmitt escorts were shot down yesterday into the sea off North Africa, the Royal Air Force announced today. Still others may have been destroyed, a communique said, with only one British 'plane lost.

(There was no word whether the German planes were carrying troops or where they were bound when the R.A.F. intercepted them. The Junkers 52's, carrying a score or more troops, have been used in all the German invasion campaigns to date, both for parachutists and for the transport of regular infantrymen to hot spots.)

In addition to the fight off North Africa, the R.A.F. reported destruction of four Messerschmitts over Malta Monday afternoon and Tuesday morning and of a Heinkel 111 over the Eastern Mediterranean on Monday. Two British fighters were listed as missing.

Informed quarters in London said the lumbering Junkers probably were carrying reinforcements of men or material from Crete to the Axis armies in North Africa or returning from such a mission.

There was no information where the planes were going to or coming from Africa.

54 Death Toll In Mine Explosion

MORGANTOWN, W. Va, May 13. — (BUP) — Rescue crews reached the bodies of 33 men in the Christopher Coal Co. Mine No. 3, today, raising to 54 the death toll of an explosion which ripped through the mine late yesterday.

Four men, a draft working, is situated at Osage, five miles from here.

Believed caused by a "gas pocket", the blast ripped through two sections of the mine with devastating force, bringing down tons of rock, coal and dirt to form a barricade behind which the victims were trapped.

Those not killed by the blast suffocated.

35 Canadians At Hong Kong War Prisoners

By The Canadian Press.

Names of 34 officers and one Civilian Auxiliary Service man were reported as unofficially listed prisoners of war in an Army casualty list today.

The men named are those mentioned in a message received by the External Affairs Department on Canadian prisoners at Hong Kong and most of them are members of the Winnipeg Grenadiers, one of the two Canadian battalions which fought there as part of the British garrison and which were overcome by the Japanese.

Concluded on Page 12, Col. 3.

Sir Gerald Campbell Relinquishing Post

LONDON, May 13. — (CP)—The Press Association said today that Sir Gerald Campbell is relinquishing his post as Director General of British Information Services in the United States.

He is to be succeeded by Harold Butler, former director of the International Labor Office, who will have the diplomatic rank of Minister.

Canadian Makes Heroic Parachute Attack in France

VICHY, May 13.—(BUP)—A lone Canadian parachutist who landed, near Langon last night with a radio transmitter and demolition material, killed several German soldiers in a rifle battle and then, with his last bullet, killed himself, officials revealed.

The Canadian came down near the demarcation line east of Bordeaux and was immediately surrounded by a score of German soldiers.

He refused to surrender, however, and started shooting. The one-sided fight lasted for some time.

Martinique Grave Issue Says Vichy

Reply Made To Demands by United States

VICHY, May 13. — (AP) —The Vichy government announced tonight that it had sent a reply to a United States note concerning Martinique which "has given rise to grave questions".

Demands by U.S.

LONDON, May 13.—(CP)—The Vichy radio broadcast tonight a statement declaring that the United States had made demands "tending to modify the status" of French possessions in the West Indies.

(BUP)—Shortly before the announcement of Laval's reply to Washington, unconfirmed reports circulated in Vichy that Germany has demanded that the Vichy Government refuse to surrender any of the 140,000 tons of French merchant ships now at Martinique.

Before permitting the ships to fall into United States or Allied hands, Germany was reported to have stated, they must be scuttled.

Stevens Tells Church Take Down Dollar Sign Replace it With Cross

VANCOUVER, May 13.—(BUP)—A former Federal Cabinet Minister today advised the Church to "take down the dollar sign and replace it with the sign of the Cross".

Addressing the British Columbia United Church Conference, H. H. Stevens, who was Minister of Trade and Commerce in the Bennett Government, accused the church of today of "inertia" in the face of human and social problems.

"We need to hear of the church militant", he said "of groups of men and women fighting for the rights of their fellow-men. We never hear of that today."

While it was not for the Church to enter actively into politics and economics, he said, it was its duty, nevertheless, to protect human rights.

Stevens charged the Church with "shutting its eyes" to the exploitation of men and women by large corporations.

The Church was the one institution that could influence Canadian opinion, he said, and added, "but it mustn't sell Christian principles for a full contribution".

Asks Injunction Against Churchill

LONDON, May 13.—(BUP)—W. R. Hipwell, one of two Independent candidates in a Salisbury byelection for Parliament, asked the High Court today for an injunction to prevent Prime Minister Winston Churchill from publicly endorsing the Government candidate.

Germans Claim 40,000 Russians Captured

Soviets Report Furious Air Battles

But Claim 'No Substantial Changes' On Front

LONDON, May 13.—(CP)—Hitler has gathered perhaps 2,000,000 of his best combat troops in the Ukraine and is reported to be using 2,000 dive bombers to smash through the Kerch Peninsula in the Crimea, but informed quarters here today discounted his claims of having driven a breach into the Russian lines.

One informed source said the Kerch attack could be regarded as the opening of a three-speared offensive in the Caucasus with other drives to be expected from Taganrog and Kharkov.

By The Canadian Press.

Hitler's Field Headquarters asserted today that, the critical five-day-old "battle to break through on the Isthmus of Kerch" in the Crimea, gateway to the Caucasus oil treasures, had been "concluded with the annihilation of Russians encircled there and the capture of 40,000 prisoners.

Heavy fighting continued. Despatches indicated that after making a breach in the Russian defences at the entrance of Kerch Peninsula, the Germans still had nearly 50 miles to go to reach Kerch city, just across the narrow Kerch Strait from the Caucasus.

Test of Offensive.

The battle, regarded as a test phase of Hitler's long – heralded Spring offensive, started last Friday along a 10-mile front on the peninsula.

While the Germans claimed a smashing victory, a Soviet midday communique reported "no substantial changes" overnight.

In a special communique, the German High Command declared: "The battle to break through on the Isthmus of Kerch has been decided. It concluded with the annihilation of enemy forces which have been overrun and encircled there.

"Pursuit of the beaten remainder of the enemy is being continued in the direction of Kerch.

The Nazi communique said that, in addition to the 40,000 Soviet prisoners – nearly three divisions – the Russians had lost 197 tanks, 586 guns, 760 warplanes and "countless other war material". DNB, German news agency, asserted that Nazi troops were thrusting "far beyond the Parpatsch positions" to the north of the Kerch peninsula and declared.

Concluded on Page 12, Col. 6.

MADE GROUP CAPTAIN.

MONCTON, N.B., May 13.—(CP)—Wing Cmdr. W. W. Brown, Officer Commanding No. 8 Service Flying Training School here, has received word of his promotion to group captain effective April 1. Born at Hamilton, Ont., he came here from Sydney, N.S., when the school opened in November, 1940.

THE WEATHER

SOME PEOPLE BLOW BUBBLES WHILE OTHERS JUST BLOW !!

FORECASTS.

Ottawa and Upper St. Lawrence Valleys: Mostly cloudy tonight and Thursday, with scattered thundershowers. Moderate to fresh winds today, becoming strong on Thursday.

Temperatures.

Port Arthur 71, 40; Parry Sound 58, 42; London 68, 51; Toronto 63, 50; Kingston 62, 47; Ottawa 59, 49; Montreal 58, 51.

BELMONT RESULTS.

First race, purse $1,500, claiming, two-year-olds, five furlongs. (W. Eads) 4.20, 2.60, 2.10; Somether; 117 (A. Robertson) 3.50, 2.40; Water Pearl, 116 (D. Meade) 2.50. Time 59 4-5. Santa Rosa, Tamlin and Budded also ran.

DR. JOHN J. ROY.

SYDNEY, N.S., May 13. — (CP)—Dr. John J. Roy, 67, who practised medicine here for 40 years, died suddenly today at his home.

Enticing Items

From Today's Want Ads

Auto radios cost $30.00 for most cars. See Articles for Sale.

Service station attendant wanted Must be efficient, energetic.

Need wedding company projects use of tents, poses, fancy blocks, etc. See Business Cards.

Electric cleaners, rebuilt and fully guaranteed, at low prices.

145. Prey! *Pennsylvanian Sun* (tanker) off Key West, Florida.

146. *Pan Massachusetts* (tanker) off Cape Canaveral, Florida.

Starting in February, the Nazis had also carried the fight to the Caribbean in a blitz on tankers. Sinkings in the North Atlantic continued and on the 10th Canada lost another ship (HMCS *Spikenard*, corvette); a torpedo struck her magazine — only eight survived. In May U-boats attacked ships in the Gulf of Mexico, striking oil and bauxite carriers that were essential to U.S. refineries and aluminum smelters. Though a maximum of only six U-boats ever operated in the Gulf, 41 ships were sunk. America introduced gasoline rationing in May, which limited consumers to a mere three gallons a week. In June Doenitz extended U-boat operations to the waters of Venezuela — a tanker-rich region — and down Brazil's coast. The latter move was undertaken in retaliation for Brazil's action in rounding up Axis sympathizers on Washington's advice — after Hitler had offered Brazil millions of dollars in return for U-boat bases. U-boat attacks prompted the Brazilians, who lost five merchant ships in five days, to declare war on Germany and on Italy (22 August 1942). The U.S. Navy secured valuable Brazilian bases, the final link in the convoy network. From September until the end of the year 1,400 ships were convoyed through the eastern system and of these only 11 were sunk.

In March the U-boat fleet had grown to 315 boats, with about 80 operating on a daily basis in the Atlantic. Doenitz, who was careful to keep operations going against the main transatlantic lifeline, was able to intensify his attacks as successes dwindled to the west and south; even in February, with "the American turkey shoot" at its height, one of his packs had sunk six ships of a westbound convoy. In the Mediterranean; also, German pressure had not relaxed. During the spring and summer vicious air and sea battles raged near and over Malta, Britain's strategic island fortress in the central Mediterranean. Since the turn of the year

the Germans had attempted to eliminate the island as a British naval and air base by sending over dense clouds of bombers — they were fully aware of the menace that air, surface and submarine forces based there posed to the German—Italian supply lines on which the Axis forces in North Africa depended. From mid-March to the end of April the German air force rendered Malta barely tenable, and Rommel, nourished by supplies, swung into the offensive at the end of May.* Hitler, with a second summer campaign in Russia looming, shrugged off pressure to commit airborne troops to seize the island at this most propitious time; he remembered Crete. Two major attempts to supply Malta, in June and in August, led to the biggest convoy battles of the Mediterranean naval war. German E-boats (motor torpedo boats) damaged the cruiser *Newcastle* and sank the destroyer *Hasty* in June; in August the carrier *Eagle* was sunk by a U-boat *(U-73)* and a second carrier, *Indomitable*, was heavily damaged by dive-bombers. Only five supply ships reached the island. But they were enough to keep Malta fighting and by the autumn the island had been resupplied.

Meanwhile there had been some activity in the Arctic. The western Allies were agreed that Russia must be furnished with supplies if she were to survive. They also knew that, in the final analysis, Hitler could only be defeated by an invasion of Europe. Brigadier General Dwight D. Eisenhower, destined to be the supreme commander of the invasion force in 1944, told McNaughton, who visited Roosevelt at the President's invitation early in 1942, that he saw no way other than by mounting an offensive from England "across the narrow

---

*In the air-fighting that summer George Frederick Beurling, a Canadian pilot serving with the RAF, destroyed 27 German and Italian aircraft, probably destroyed three more, and damaged eight. His record on the island was never surpassed.

147. A Malta-bound convoy under air attack from Sicily, August 1942.

material, the British planners were convinced that no successful invasion could be launched in 1942. The Americans felt otherwise and so, often insultingly, did Stalin. In April General Marshall went to London. The British went so far as to agree to an emergency cross-Channel attack in 1942 should the Russian situation deteriorate so badly as to warrant it; and this would be followed by a major invasion in 1943. Monster passenger liners, such as the *Queen Elizabeth* and the *Queen Mary* (which could each carry 10,000 servicemen across the Atlantic), sailed independently, their speed of some 30 knots being counted on to give them safety. They ran the U-boat gauntlet successfully throughout the war. Britain accepted a cut of 250,000 tons of imports to help the American build-up and the British ration had to be reduced still further (in bulk, at any rate, though

148. *Queen Mary* carries American troops to Britain.

seas'' and McNaughton emphatically agreed. The proper timing of this strategy caused concern. Faced with shipping losses, and the primary requisite of a massive build-up of both men and

concentrated foods ensured that the calorie level was maintained). The sending of reinforcements to the Middle East was also affected, though the Russia-bound convoys still continued to ply the Arctic seas.

U-boats were already in Arctic waters at the beginning of 1942 (as well as the Mediterranean) despite Doenitz's conviction that they should have been concentrated in what he always considered to be the vital theatre — the North Atlantic. Submarines, as well as ships, fighting the winter storms in those latitudes found it extremely hard to operate. Though ships had been carrying goods to Russia since the summer of 1941, the first U-boat kill did not come until January 1942 when *U-132* sank the 5,000-ton *Waziristan*.

Hitler ordered heavy ships to northern Norway. In March 1942 *Tirpitz* (sister ship of *Bismarck* and equally powerful) had completed and lay ready for action in the Faetten Fjord, near Trondheim. With the pocket battleship *Scheer*, the heavy cruiser *Hipper* and destroyers, Hitler now had a northern fleet whose purpose he stated in a directive dated 14 March:

. . . the enemy depends on sustaining Russia's ability to hold out by maximum deliveries of war material and provisions, and at the same time to set up a second European front . . . an enemy landing on the Norwegian Arctic coast must be regarded as likely. . . . For this reason it is necessary that maritime communications over the Arctic Ocean between the Anglo-Saxons and Russia, hitherto virtually unimpeded, should henceforth be impeded.

proposed it formally on 2 June, but the scheme (Operation "Jupiter") was rejected by the British Chiefs of Staff. On 9 July Churchill directed McNaughton — in a move that was unconstitutional to say the least — to review his Chiefs' decision, placing at his disposal every scrap of intelligence that was available. The Canadian troops in Britain would provide the bulk of the invading force, a force designed to free the "aid to Russia" route around the North Cape of Norway from German interference, thereby saving hundreds of lives, many precious ships and thousands of tons of equipment and supplies. A successful invasion would, in fact, establish a second front adjacent to the Russians (Norway, in the north, has a common frontier with Russia), from which, in Churchill's words, "if the going was good we could advance gradually southward, unrolling the Nazi map of Europe from the top". It would, moreover, satisfy to some extent the clamour of public opinion in North America and Britain — Lord Beaverbrook resigned from the cabinet because of British failure to open a second front in Europe in 1942 — and perhaps prevent Germany (through increased supplies to Russia) from inflicting such defeats on the Soviets that they would be forced to capitulate. And that was important at this stage of the war.

"Jupiter" would be no small affair: the naval

149. Submarines, as well as ships, found it hard to operate in Arctic latitudes.
a. On the bridge of a destroyer.

150. b. The iced-up deckgun of a U-boat.

The fleet, then, had to stand by to frustrate an Allied invasion, and it also had to attack the Murmansk convoys.

That directive is a revelation of Hitler's remarkable intuition; alone of all the Allied leaders, Churchill was indeed turning over the possibilities of invading northern Norway at the time. He

requirements included four battleships, an aircraft-carrier, 15 cruisers, four heavy monitors, 52 destroyers, 22 corvettes, 48 minesweepers and a host of smaller craft to support convoys, carrying troops and their supplies, consisting of 150 ships and 450 assault landing craft of various types. The air force would provide 21 squadrons — mostly fighter — to counteract the German bombers. The invasion force (two corps plus one division, with

151. *Tirpitz*.

152. In Arctic waters.
a. Escort

153. b. Convoy

support units) would number 116,000 men; and there would be a follow-up force of one division. Churchill was set on using three Canadian divisions out of five initially required, for Canadians "naturally knew about arctic warfare"; and he thought "the operation would give a glorious opportunity to the Canadian Army which had for two years been eating its heart out in Britain awaiting the invader". McNaughton, after a cool review, pointed out to Churchill that there was little possibility of achieving surprise, and that success would depend on a combination of weather conditions against which the odds would be about six to one in December (the month proposed for the attack). At this point Churchill looked quizzically at McNaughton over the top of his spectacles. "I sometimes envy Stalin," he said. "He can shoot those who disagree with him." Perhaps so, replied McNaughton, but democracy had some advantages too; "masters, as well as servants, could give up office without being shot". Churchill conceded that there might be something in that.

Churchill still considered that an invasion would be feasible with Russian help, and he proposed sending McNaughton to Moscow to draw up a joint plan with Stalin. This he suggested to Mackenzie King, but the Canadian Prime Minister, who wanted no prominent part for Canada either politically or militarily, poured cold water on the whole idea — though his misgivings, as he put it, would not be so strong were McNaughton to be a member, though not the head, of a combined mission to include British and American representatives. "I am sorry about McNaughton," Churchill replied by cable, "I thought that at this critical juncture in Anglo-American relations with the Soviets his personality and knowledge of the subject might have got a good plan worked out with the Russians. . . . Moreover, as Commander-in-Chief of the Canadian Army he would no doubt have got access to Stalin himself which will probably not be the case with any British general." So the idea of "Jupiter" was shelved but not forgotten; Churchill revived it at his meeting with Roosevelt at Quebec in 1943 as an alternative should a cross-Channel assault prove impracticable.

In March, during a foray by *Tirpitz* to tackle a convoy of 16 ships, the Germans got wind of a British battle squadron with one carrier, and the battleship turned back. *Tirpitz* was attacked by Albacore torpedo-bombers and was lucky to escape; the British lost two aircraft. This alarmed Raeder, who had no aircraft carrier, and he appealed to Hitler for *Luftwaffe* support: it was this that brought German reconnaisance, bomber and torpedo aircraft to fields in northern Norway.

In April German U-boats and destroyers tackled a 25-ship convoy (PQ 15) bound from Iceland to

154. Carrying supplies to Russia.

Murmansk and a returning convoy of 13 ships (QP 11) that was steaming in the opposite direction. During the ensuing battle, fought in a stiff nor'easter that drove blinding snow across the towering seas, the British lost one cruiser and one destroyer for one German destroyer sunk; but the merchantmen, with the exception of one Russian freighter, got through.

The next convoy (PQ 16 of 25 fully-laden ships) was not so lucky. On 27 May it came within range of the *Luftwaffe*, which attacked it with more than 100 bombers. Eight ships (43,000 tons) were lost.

For six months of the year there is almost perpetual darkness in these northern latitudes, and while this provided some security it was also a time of winter gales, mountainous seas, ice, and fog for days on end; for the other half of the year the sun, which during winter barely tops the horizon, begins to climb for longer and longer periods to give, in June, perpetual day. There was no respite, in summer, from enemy attack. Convoys took from 10 to 14 days and were subjected during a large part of the voyage to air and U-boat attack from bases in northern Norway. Land-based aircraft could give support from Iceland or Britain only for the early part of the voyage when, unfortunately, it was least

needed. Losses were bound to be heavy.

Hitler sent *Lützow* to join *Scheer* in Norwegian waters. With both pocket battleships now in the far north, Raeder concluded that a decisive success could be achieved over the next convoy (PQ 17) by mounting a full-scale attack with his four large ships. The operation would be named *Rösselsprung* (Knight's Leap).

On 1 July the 34 ships of PQ 17 were spotted by German air reconnaissance. The convoy's heavy covering force (the Home Fleet) was found cruising far to the west, off Iceland — too far west, it seemed, to interfere. In these favourable conditions Raeder ordered the northern fleet to bases farther north, in Alten Fjord, where it would be well placed for attack. *Tirpitz, Hipper* and four destroyers left Trondheim; *Scheer, Lützow* and six destroyers moved out of the Narvik area. *Lützow*, however, ran aground in fog and took no further part in the operation, as did three destroyers accompanying *Tirpitz*. The British Admiralty knew that an attack on the convoy with heavy ships would have to be reckoned with, for on 3 July a reconnaissance aircraft had photographed the Germans' berths at Trondheim and found them empty. But German long-range aircraft had lost track of the powerful British Home Fleet and, until its whereabouts was

155. Submarines ranged north —

156. to attack Arctic convoys.

known, the ships were held in Alten Fjord; Hitler, who feared the loss of capital ships, had imposed caution. The Admiralty, unaware of this, thought that the *Tirpitz* and the other ships might tear into the convoy and its close escort in a matter of hours, long before the Home Fleet (which was guarding against the possible eventuality of a breakout by the large German ships into the Atlantic) could intervene. Thus, on 4 July, the Admiralty issued the orders that sealed convoy PQ 17's fate — "Cruiser force [with the convoy] to withdraw westward" and "Owing to threat of surface ships convoy is to disperse and proceed to Russian ports". The message "Most immediate — Convoy is to scatter" followed some ten minutes later.

CONVOY IS TO SCATTER

Signal 50

NAVAL MESSAGE

From: KEPPEL   To: SOMALI

Captain to Captain: What part of the bloody War Plan is this.

(T.O.O. about 2015/4)

157. The captain of *Keppel* (destroyer) protests the order — that the convoy scatter — to *Somali* (destroyer escort leader).

Signal 54

NAVAL MESSAGE

From: KEPPEL   To: COMMODORE

Sorry to leave you like this. Goodbye and good luck. It looks like a bloody business.

- - - - - - - - - - -

158. Once the convoy had scattered, the destroyers could do little to protect the individual merchant ships. The captain of *Keppel* admits as much in his message to the merchant commodore.

Deprived of defence save destroyers, which could do little once the convoy had scattered, the ships were at the mercy of the Germans; U-boats and the *Luftwaffe* sank the helpless merchantmen one after the other in a battle that lasted a week. Though the heavy German warships put to sea on the 5th they played no part in the slaughter. British reconnaissance sighted *Tirpitz* once by submarine and again by aircraft, and the reports were monitored as usual by German naval intelligence. Raeder, still unsure of the whereabouts of the Home Fleet, immediately ordered the withdrawal of his ships. Twenty-three merchantmen were sunk (two-thirds of the total) and the bed of the Barents Sea littered with their cargoes — 430 tanks, 210 aircraft and 99,316 tons of vehicles and supplies,

159. 23 Merchantmen were sunk —

160. Two thirds of the convoy.

161. A U-boat knifes through its victim's cargo.

manufactured and transported thus far at tremendous cost. Men who leaped from many of the sinking ships plunged into a "baked Alaska" of freezing water covered with blazing oil — and 150 lost their lives. Others, picked up by the destroyers and Soviet rescue vessels, were maimed by a combination of burns and frostbite from the icy sea.

It is clear that the Admiralty panicked on this occasion, causing it momentarily to forget the lessons that the Atlantic war had taught — that ships must be kept together under the protection of strong escorts at all times. On the other hand, in the German warships — which had been paralyzed into inactivity by over-caution — morale sank into a spirit of gloom and frustration.

Even before this disaster the Soviets, and the Americans, had increased their pressure on the British to open a second front across the Channel that summer. The spread of Japanese conquests seemed impossible to check, and U.S. politicians and chiefs-of-staff faced a powerful lobby urging a concentration in the Pacific. On 17 June Churchill flew to Washington to confer with Roosevelt and, above all, to protect the previously-agreed strategy of "Hitler first, then Japan". His task was made no easier in Washington by the receipt of a cable, which Roosevelt presented, advising him of the loss of the North African port of Tobruk and its garrison of 33,000 men. Little stood between Rommel and the major base at Alexandria, with Suez a short way beyond. Churchill confessed that it was "one of the heaviest blows I can recall during the war". Nevertheless, much came out of this second Washington conference that was in Britain's favour — no major cross-Channel invasion before 1943 (save, as we have seen, if Russia's position were to deteriorate so badly as to warrant an "emergency" invasion in 1942) and, in the meantime, a joint American/British invasion of North Africa, from the west, towards the end of 1942. The Allies were, in fact, in no way ready to carry out an invasion of Northwest Europe that year — or, as it turned out, in 1943. It proved practicable only to mount the Dieppe raid in August before Allied offensive preparations concentrated on the invasion of North Africa.

Churchill faced a censure of his direction of the war in the House of Commons on 1 July, after his return to London. He was not only Prime Minister; he was also Minister of Defence. It was confidently predicted, in the press, that he would be relieved as Defence minister by McNaughton of Canada, whose "decisive practical mind" had already exerted considerable influence on defence planning. Sir George Schuster, during the debate, pointed to the need "for fighting knowledge, mechanical knowledge and scientific vision all combined. I wonder whether it might not be advisable to get a man like General McNaughton?" The motion of censure was heavily defeated. But on 9 July McNaughton was approached informally, at Churchill's instigation, to "take over the direction of technical development for all three services, army, navy and air force, as a member of the British Government". McNaughton refused to consider it, stating that he was responsible to the Canadian government for the First Canadian Army, which he then commanded.

He commanded the Army when, on 19 August, the 2nd Canadian Division raided Dieppe, a reconnaissance in force that was designed to test the German defences on the coast of France — a prerequisite for planning the full-scale invasion of Northwest Europe that would come. The Royal Canadian Navy, despite heavy commitments to the Atlantic struggle, helped man the landing craft flotillas that carried the troops to shore. The raid was costly (3,367 casualties, all ranks) but it served its purpose; the lessons learned saved countless Allied lives in the grand-scale invasion of Normandy in 1944, which, without Dieppe, could easily have been a fiasco.

Arctic convoys, suspended for a time, resumed with PQ 18 in September. Larger than its predecessor, it lost 13 ships (a third of its total) to air and U-boat attacks. This time a strengthened escort remained with the merchantmen and gave as good as it got. In October and November, when all available transports were committed to the landings in North Africa, only single ships sailed for Murmansk. Hardly were the transports back from Africa when they were again loaded with material for Russia. The first of these convoys bore the letters JW instead of the unlucky PQ and was numbered 51. It was split into two sections. The first section, JW 51A, of 16 ships, sailed from Scotland on 15 December and, screened by the polar night, reached Murmansk safely on the 25th. It carried 100,000 tons of war supplies — a welcome Christmas gift for Stalin's armies.

The second section, JW 51B, which had sailed on the 14th, was, however, spotted from the air. It prompted Operation *Regenbogen* (Rainbow) — an interception by *Hipper, Lützow* and six destroyers, which Hitler authorized when he was told that the escort was weak. These ships steamed through Alten Fjord and by early morning on 31 December they had split to search for the convoy, which was escorted by five destroyers; two cruisers, *Sheffield* and *Jamaica*, farther out, provided extra cover. Darkness gave way to polar dawn when, in a grey veil, *Hipper* blundered upon the destroyer *Onslow*, which it damaged with a devastating salvo, leaving 40 dead and wounded on the decks. *Onslow* withdrew to the convoy behind smoke and the destroyer screen remained in place. Some time

162. Canadian landing craft at Dieppe, 19 August 1942.

later, in gloom and snow, *Hipper* struck the destroyer *Achates*, which began to sink. At this point *Sheffield* and *Jamaica* joined the fight, striking *Hipper* with 6-inch shells that set the aircraft hangar ablaze and destroyed a boiler room, which cut down the cruiser's speed. A German destroyer swerved in to be practically blown out of the water by seven salvoes delivered at close quarters. The damaged *Hipper* disengaged and *Lützow*, after damaging the destroyer *Obdurate*, did the same. The convoy reached Murmansk, thanks to the action of the destroyers, without loss.

164. *Lützow* (formerly *Deutschland*).

163. *Admiral Hipper* (heavy cruiser).

The German warships, observing strict radio silence, reached Alten Fjord on New Year's Day,

the crew of *Hipper* fighting desperately to secure the remaining engine room from water that was pouring in from the damaged section. Land communications had broken down and no report could be made to Berlin. Hitler, confidently expecting the destruction of the convoy — thus bringing relief to his armies on the Eastern Front, where the destruction of the Sixth Army at Stalingrad was almost certain — waited impatiently for confirmation. He was not accustomed to being kept waiting, or to being kept

1942

in the dark. But no word came. Finally, to his fury, an aide brought him a copy of a British Reuters news release: Heavy German forces had attacked a weakly-protected convoy in the Barents Sea but had been driven off with no loss to the convoy. One German destroyer had been sunk and a cruiser damaged. The Admiralty regretted to announce the loss of HMS *Achates*. This, as we shall see, prompted Hitler to replace Raeder as Grand Admiral with the effective Doenitz.

While Doenitz was racking up a shipping-score in the Caribbean and the Gulf of Mexico of 750,000 tons, the Allies at least gained a respite on the all-important northern Atlantic routes. The early summer saw convoys steaming back and forth on long transatlantic voyages that were almost immune from U-boats.

In July, however, with the new U.S. convoy system working well, Doenitz concentrated his forays further south until, with Brazil at war, the Americans began to operate from Brazilian and other South Atlantic bases. In September *U-156* torpedoed and sank the liner *Laconia*, which, unfortunately for the Axis, was carrying 1,800 Italian prisoners of war from North Africa around the Cape to Britain*. The U-boat, which began a rescue operation, reported to Doenitz by radio and also requested help, ''in clear'', on the international wave band. Other U-boats hastened to the scene — as did U.S. bombers from Ascension, which attacked *U-156*, though unsuccessfully. As a consequence Doenitz ordered that, in future, no rescue attempts would be made by U-boats; for this he was indicted, after the war, as a war criminal at Nüremberg.

Pickings for U-boats in these waters were no longer easy. Nor, Doenitz feared, would they be in the North Atlantic, for the Allied escorts had increased in numbers, aircraft were more effective and radar, with Huff-Duff, was a growing threat. Already, in July, when some U-boats had returned to their former hunting grounds, the stronger escort groups had struck hard. HMCS *St. Croix* (one of the old ex-American destroyers) had, on the 24th, depth-charged and sunk *U-90* after a two-hour hunt. A week later two Canadian warships — *Skeena*, part of Canada's pre-war destroyer fleet, and the corvette *Wetaskiwin* (''Wet-Ass-Queen'') — sank *U-588* after an even longer asdic hunt. *Skeena*'s depth charges did the final damage; *Wetaskiwin* screened her while she picked up the grisly evidence of the kill. And on 6 August HMCS *Assiniboine* (a second destroyer of the pre-war fleet) twice rammed and then depth-charged *U-210* in a spectacular encounter that was recorded on canvas

*The *Empress of Canada*, also carrying prisoners, suffered a like fate off Sierra Leone in March 1943.

by war artist Harold Beament. The destroyer, blazing amidships, and under fire from the U-boat's close-range weapons, is depicted as it swung round to ram.

165. HMCS *St. Croix*.

166. *HMCS* Assiniboine *versus U-boat*, by Harold Beament.

Lieutenant Ralph Hennessy, with cool determination, set about controlling the blaze; in the wheelhouse Chief Petty Officer Max Bernays carried out helm and engine room orders despite the raging inferno outside, which licked the glass. On the bridge Lieutenant-Commander John Stubbs held *Assiniboine* close to the weaving U-boat, permitting one of the destroyer's 4.7-inch guns to score a direct hit on the conning tower and her machine-guns to rake the deck. The submarine desperately attempted to dive. Stubbs at last had a reasonably steady target. He rammed, the destroyer recoiled, and he rammed again. Depth charges, and a shell from an after gun, made the kill certain. The

U-boat sank, head down, in no more than a couple of minutes.

Nevertheless, the U-boat fleet was almost at the 300-boat level considered necessary for a really decisive blow, and 30 boats were being added every month. Doenitz decided on an autumn "convoy-war", and for that he would set up patrol lines on either side of the 300-mile-wide mid-Atlantic air gap that still existed, so as to intercept convoys that were steaming east or west, subjecting them to attacks by wolf packs from one side of the black pit to the other. In that area U-boats, secure from attack, could run on the surface in daylight; and here they could refuel from milch cows in safety. Pouncing as a group on a convoy just outside the limits of Iceland-based aircraft, they would harry it until what ships were left gained the protection of aircraft based in Newfoundland. They would then withdraw, replenish with fuel, torpedoes and supplies from the milch cows, and return to the edge of the gap to wait for an eastbound convoy.

The results, from the German point of view, were impressive. From the first week of August to the end of November, when winter gales of

167. John Stubbs (when lieutenant) on the bridge of *Assiniboine* earlier in the war. Commodore G.C. Jones is on his right.

168. A "milch cow" (supply submarine) replenishes at Bordeaux.

169. U-boats on their way to set up patrol lines in mid-Atlantic.

1942

170. HMCS *Ottawa*.

171. Landing craft in use during the Allied invasion of North Africa.

extraordinary ferocity temporarily slowed the sinkings, the Allies lost almost two million tons of shipping. In November alone 119 merchantmen (729,160 tons) were lost. For Canada a westbound convoy (which lost nine ships) in September was memorable. One of the escorts, HMCS *Ottawa* (another member of Canada's destroyer fleet at the outbreak of war), had her bows blown off while investigating an asdic contact and was sunk shortly afterwards by a second torpedo with the greatest loss so far. The boats went down with her. Five

officers and 109 men perished, many of them — crowding the few rafts that had floated clear — from exposure. A later convoy (SL 125), harried from one side of the black pit to the other at the end of October, lost 12 merchantmen in the biggest convoy battle of the month; but the sacrifice, in this case, was more than offset by the fact that the convoy had attracted a group of southbound U-boats away from the large troop-carrying convoys that were then at sea for the invasion of North Africa; and ten U-boats, stationed west of Gibraltar, were despatched by Doenitz to Madeira to attack a northbound convoy. In all, convoys comprising some 350 merchant ships, supported by 200 warships, converged on North Africa almost entirely unmolested by U-boats. They delivered 70,000 men and their equipment to the North

172. Men and vehicles hit the beach.

African coast. The RCN, as at Dieppe, took part in these operations. Canadian landing craft flotillas ferried both American and British troops landing close to Algiers. Canadian corvettes — 16 of them — helped escort the convoys to North Africa, and three of these ships, working with supply convoys, sank submarines. *Port Arthur* and *Regina* accounted for one Italian submarine apiece while *Ville de Québec* sank *U-224*. Two corvettes were lost, *Louisburg* by an aerial torpedo and *Weyburn* through striking a mine. Canadian-born Frederick Thornton Peters, a captain in the Royal Navy, won the Victoria Cross at Oran for an attempt to force the boom defences in the face of point blank fire from shore batteries, a destroyer and a cruiser; blinded in one eye, he alone of the officers and men on the bridge survived, and his ship, HMS *Walney*, was a blazing wreck.

Ville de Québec's action, which was all over in ten minutes, had been full of drama. Her depth charges blew the bow of the U-boat clean out of the water; then the submarine smacked back, flat on the surface. The corvette's guns blasted the conning tower as the ship closed to ram. She caught the U-boat between conning tower (which was seen to be full of dead and wounded men) and the forward gun, which was torn from its mounting. The U-boat

sank by the bow, her stern — with rudder and propellers visible — rearing sharply out of the water before the boat slid beneath the surface. *Port Arthur* straddled her victim with depth charges; the submarine surfaced, but before the ship could close the Italian crew scuttled the boat. *Regina*, accounting for the other Italian submarine, brought it to the surface with depth charges and then, in a running battle, sank it with the 4-inch gun; 21 prisoners were taken, many of them badly wounded. As for the ships that were sunk, *Louisburg* went down with 38 men, *Weyburn* with seven.

The Anglo-American landings on the morning of 8 November at Casablanca, Oran and near Algiers — coming hard on General Sir Bernard Montgomery's (British Eighth Army) victory over Rommel at El Alamein and his subsequent westward drive — marked the turning point of the Mediterranean war, which was to steadily undermine the Axis. With French North Africa under seige, Hitler hastily moved into Vichy France on the opposite side of the Mediterranean Sea. The Vichyites, in retaliation, scuttled the remaining

173. An Italian submarine of the type sunk by the Canadian corvettes *Port Arthur* and *Regina*.

174. The North African landings — Operation TORCH
ships en route.

175. The landings near Algiers. Six Canadian landing
craft flotillas delivered both American and British
troops ashore.

176. A U-boat crew, leaving a French base for the North Atlantic, waves goodbye. At the end of 1942 U-boats were still winning the tonnage war.

heavy warships of the French fleet at Toulon, thus removing that surviving menace to the Allies.

Nevertheless, the Battle of the Atlantic in 1942 ended with the Germans well ahead. They were still winning the tonnage war. World-wide losses from all causes (mainly U-boats) reached the staggering total for the year of eight million tons. Despite new construction, there was a net loss of more than a million tons. Eighty-seven U-boats had been sunk — more than twice the 1941 figure — but by the end of the year operational U-boat strength stood at 212, with another 181 undergoing trials and 70 new boats being commissioned every quarter. There could be no hope of Britain's survival, let alone a future invasion of Northwest Europe from the British Isles, if the present pattern were to continue.

A worried Churchill set up an "Anti-U-boat Warfare" Committee, which first met in November 1942. At these meetings it was obvious to the First

177. The interior of what were believed to be bomb-proof U-boat pens at Trondheim, Norway. From Trondheim the U-boats were close to the North Atlantic as well as to Arctic waters.

Sea Lord, Admiral Sir Dudley Pound, that the first thing to do would be to provide more very long-range aircraft to patrol the centre of the North Atlantic, then devoid of cover, where the heaviest losses were taking place.* Air Marshal "Bomber" Harris, chief of RAF Bomber Command, opposed this view. He claimed that the best way to kill U-boats was at their source — the industrial plants in Germany that built them — and by raids against their coastal bases. But in fact Harris had left the bombing of the Biscay ports until far too late. The Germans, alive to the danger, had put their U-boats and maintenance facilities under reinforced concrete shelters with bomb-proof roofs that were tremendously thick. The U.S. air force had attacked Lorient with Fortresses and Liberators in October, scoring direct hits with 2,000-pound bombs on the concrete roofs. The bombs failed to break through. In later offensives by both British and U.S. aircraft on this and other submarine bases, not a single U-boat was lost. Nor was production affected; despite hundreds of sorties and the dropping of thousands of tons of bombs (with the consequent losses of aircraft and their crews), the Germans were to state that up to this time not a single U-boat had been prevented from entering service. Harris would not relinquish to Coastal Command any of the Liberators that were badly needed; nor any of the U.S. 10-cm ASV sets. Both Churchill and Roosevelt favoured the bomber offensive as the most direct way of bringing aid to Russia — and as a counterweight to Stalin's insistent demand for a second front in Europe "now".

Nevertheless, the committee did agree that the Atlantic air gap must be closed. The Admiralty reported that the new escort carriers — from which aircraft could fly and return — would not be operational before the spring of 1943. Churchill, therefore, made a personal appeal to Roosevelt on 20 November for 30 Liberators with the new "centimetre" ASV equipment that was Metox proof. Yet by February the British were flying only 23, including those already in service, and few of these had the new-type radar. American production was not yet in full stride; by the end of the year it was no more than that of Britain and Canada combined, and a large part of it was going to Russia. But the trickle of new ships and American armaments had become a steady flow. Backed by the industrial power of the United States, it would become a flood, and the Germans knew that the Battle of the Atlantic would have to be won quickly if it were to be won at all. Both sides entered 1943 with the full knowledge that this would be the crucial year.

178. A Mosquito aircraft attacks a U-boat with rockets. During the war a thousand Mosquitoes were built in Canada. A fine aircraft, it did not have the range to close the Atlantic gap in air-cover.

*Only one Coastal Command squadron, which sank its first U-boat in October, had Liberators at the time and these were equipped with metre-wave ASV (radar) developed by the British. The Germans fitted an antidote in the form of the "Metox" detector — a receiver capable of detecting these radar transmissions; it emitted a high-pitched buzz when subjected to the radar probe of an approaching aircraft and so enabled the U-boat to escape. The Americans, however, had developed a 10-cm microwave radar against which the U-boats' search receivers were ineffective.

The war within a war

Before turning to 1943 it is necessary to briefly review another battle that had been fought ever since the outbreak of war. This was the struggle between the naval intelligence organizations of Germany and Britain for the supremacy that would give the edge to one side or the other in the Atlantic battle. It resolved itself, basically, into the reading by one of the other's transmitted messages and thus was a matter of breaking codes and ciphers.

The Germans had the advantage in 1939. Their naval cryptanalysis service, the *B. Dienst*, had penetrated the British naval ciphers — manual tables — at the time of the Abyssinian War, and when the Second World War broke out they were able to decrypt operational messages. They had a clear idea of British shipping movements until August 1940, when changes were made in the ciphers which defeated them for a time. The German "enigma" machine ciphers remained secure throughout this period. At the time of the German seaborne invasion of Norway, for example, the *B. Dienst* provided first-class intelligence concerning British movements. British Intelligence, on the other hand, could not give the firm advance warning that would have permitted counter-measures to be taken against the German invasion fleet.

Despite the change in British ciphers after August 1940, the *B. Dienst*, though deprived of knowledge of Home Fleet movements, still managed to decipher convoy signals. This, as Doenitz admitted, greatly assisted wolf pack tactics at a time when U-boats were in short supply. Submarines could be in the right place at the right time and the contribution of the *B. Dienst* has been estimated as being worth an extra 50 boats.

British Intelligence had begun to read German *Luftwaffe* and army traffic as early as April 1940,

and this too was machine-ciphered. Naval machines contained technical modifications, however, and were more secure. The German navy, moreover, had no fewer than 13 ciphers, of which HYDRA, used at first by all operational U-boats, may be mentioned. HYDRA was later changed to TRITON for operational U-boats in the Atlantic; those in the Mediterranean or Norway used other ciphers. The British realized that only the capture of a naval machine, with current settings, could provide the starting point. On 8 May 1941, *U-110*, commanded by Fritz Lemp (who had sunk the passenger liner *Athenia*), was captured intact, providing the machine that was needed. Forced to the surface, and with a destroyer swerving in to ram, Lemp and his crew jumped into the water. But the destroyer sheered off, picked up the crew, and then despatched a boarding party to the U-boat. Lemp, who had been missed by the rescuers, saw what was happening; he started to swim towards the submarine to scuttle it before it could be boarded. He was spotted and shot. The party recovered the machine, its current daily setting, and spare rotor wheels to give British Intelligence the start that was so desperately required. They quickly penetrated Doenitz's HYDRA traffic, though there were gaps when settings were periodically changed.

As early as mid-May 1941 the reading of German traffic enabled the British to round up *Bismarck*'s supply fleet of six tankers, stationed in various Atlantic areas. All were either captured, sunk or scuttled. That these widely spread ships should have been pinpointed with such uncanny accuracy was obviously suspicious to the Germans, who staged an inquiry; it placed the blame, not on compromised codes and cipher tables, but on operational instructions that must have been found on one of the captured ships. "Merchant" surface

179. The map in the Operations Room, Western Approaches (Liverpool) on which the current situation of the Battle of the Atlantic (including the positions of convoys, escorts and enemy vessels) was shown.

raiders and supply ships for the U-boats could also be tracked down and disposed of — as they were; Doenitz concluded that supply would in future have to be by submarine tankers (his milch cows), as we have seen. The U-boats themselves, however — though the British were able to build up a very comprehensive knowledge of the operational U-boat fleet, its dispositions and its movements — were much more elusive than surface ships; but at least some successful diversions of convoys could be made. As a result of these, shipping losses fell in July and August. They rose again in the fall, when the U-boats, aided by air reconnaissance, were mauling the Gibraltar convoys.

The secrets obtained from *U-110* enabled the British to predict the U-boat offensive against U.S. shipping off the eastern seaboard with great accuracy; it is incomprehensible that the Americans, who were advised, ignored the warning

as they did. That, however, was the last major coup with HYDRA: on 1 February 1942 the Germans scrapped HYDRA and switched to TRITON, an entirely new cipher that completely baffled the British until the end of the year. The blackout was total. But the reading of HYDRA for so long had given the British an insight into Doenitz's mind. They knew the way he operated; some of his moves could be predicted. And knowledge of HYDRA enabled the British to finally break into TRITON; it also led to success with other ciphers, notably NEPTUN, governing the operations of the heavy ships, which was to be of great importance later.

The British ciphers for heavy ships, changed towards the end of 1940, had been unbuttoned by the Germans in the summer of 1942. And movement orders issued to convoys once they were at sea played into the Germans' hands at a time when intelligence about U-boat movements was not

180. *U-107* takes on fuel from the supply ship *Nordmark* in the South Atlantic. The breaking of German codes enabled the British to dispose of this and other vessels.

The War Within a War

available. The *B. Dienst* was of enormous help to Doenitz in his fall offensive and it is remarkable that any convoy passed through without being intercepted. Decrypting, however, was not always fast enough to be effective. When 1943 opened the *B. Dienst* continued, as always, to decrypt convoy routing signals and was working with full efficiency. It could detect evasive diversions and so permit Doenitz to counteract the British moves. Thus, with the British at last reading TRITON, save for a brief period in March, 1943, when the Germans activated another rotor in their "enigma" machines, it would seem that the odds were at least even in the intelligence war during what turned out to be the crucial phase of the Atlantic battle. It was always important to strike a correct balance between making the best use of the knowledge obtained, and not arousing the suspicions of the other side that its ciphers had been compromised. Nevertheless both sides did become suspicious — the Germans when their patrols did not find the convoys for which they were searching; the British when diversions failed to draw convoys out of danger. The British, in May, again changed their codes so that from June 1943 until the end of the war the *B. Dienst* was never able to furnish Doenitz with more than a trickle of information about convoy routings. The Germans checked and re-checked their ciphers but still concluded that TRITON was unbreakable. Thus, while the British had the advantage from June 1943 onwards, for the first half of 1943 neither side had the edge over the other; claims that "Ultra" — the intelligence derived through reading German messages — made it possible for the Allies to win the Battle of the Atlantic during this period are clearly incorrect.

181. The diversion of a convoy, to avoid U-boats, as seen from the air.

The War Within a War

1943
The Atlantic war is won

Events occurred in January 1943 in both the Axis and Allied camps that were to influence the impending decisive phase of the Atlantic tonnage war.

In mid-month Churchill and Roosevelt held a war conference, their third, at Casablanca with military advisers present. Decisions of far-reaching importance were made. First, the winning of the campaign against U-boats in the Atlantic was at last recognized as having absolute priority. This would facilitate the build-up of American forces in Britain, which should be done as rapidly as possible. The bombing of Germany would be extended to include daylight attacks by the Americans, which, with British night operations, would subject the Reich to bombing around the clock. Planning would start for a cross-Channel attack in 1944. There was some argument about the next decision — that the invasion of Sicily would follow the clearing of North Africa. The British wanted either Sicily or Sardinia, and preferably the latter, as a prelude to invading Italy. The Americans, while recognizing that a cross-Channel invasion was probably unrealistic in 1943, did not want to get embroiled in the Mediterranean in the meantime. Churchill stood for Sicily, and Roosevelt agreed with him. At the end of the conference Roosevelt, much to the consternation of Churchill, who had not been consulted, announced to the press that the Allies would settle for nothing less than the "unconditional surrender" of the Axis partners, a decision that undoubtedly prolonged the war. Churchill, in the interests of solidarity, did not demur. Because no terms would be considered, the Nazis kept the German people in thrall long after any prospect of victory had disappeared.

Shortly after this 10-day conference — on 30 January — Doenitz replaced Raeder as commander-in-chief of the entire German navy. Furious at the failure of *Lützow* and *Hipper* to destroy the Russia-bound convoy at the end of 1942, Hitler had condemned the heavy ships as "completely useless". They would be paid off and reduced to scrap, their guns mounted on land for coastal defence. That, he raged, was his "unalterable resolve", and he sacked Raeder from the post he had held for 15 years. The hard-headed Doenitz managed to preserve the ships — whose scrapping would have been a cheap victory for the Allies — but used his new powers to lavish all the naval resources at his disposal on the U-boat service.

182. Churchill and Roosevelt, with their military advisers, meet at Casablanca.

183. Doenitz, the new head of the German navy.

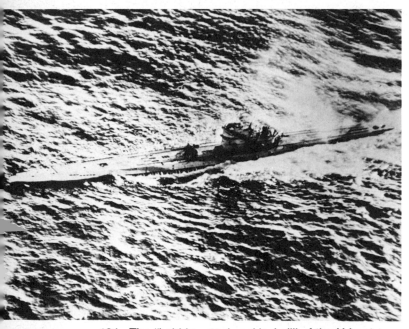

184. The "bobbing steel cockleshell" of the U-boat.

January, because of even worse weather than in 1941, brought shipping losses of only 200,000 tons. Inside "the bobbing steel cockleshells" of the U-boats, as one submariner put it, there was the stench of vomit and diesel oil; clothes, even food, reeked of oil. Visibility was blotted out and many convoys forged through the patrol lines unseen. Some weather-worn ships, buffeted by the storms, dropped sickeningly into the troughs between the massive waves and broke apart. Others, beset by weather, straggled out of the orderly convoy

columns — easy victims in U-boat infested seas.

Doenitz now had 400 boats and he was able to station 120 operationally in the Atlantic — as far as the Cape routes off Africa and with a powerful concentration to cover the Gibraltar routes. His main battleground, however, was still the black pit and in that relatively small area he had fifty boats.

To protect the all-important merchant ships — salt-caked and rusty for the most part, though some were newly-built — the Allies deployed destroyers, frigates, sloops and American cutters as well as aircraft: Liberators, Fortresses, Sunderlands, Catalinas and Hudsons. There were about seventy corvettes, still badly needed, and new frigates were appearing. These — twin-screw corvettes — were faster and therefore more effective. An increasing number of ships had been fitted with the "hedgehog", a multiple mortar mounted forward capable of launching 24 bombs at a time; they exploded on contact and were lethal. Thus a ship holding a submarine in its asdic beam could attack as it approached the target without losing asdic contact — an advantage over the stern-mounted depth-charge throwers. Goodeve, who once again was behind the development of the new weapon, offered a bottle of sherry for the best name. He liked "hedgehog", with its suggestion of prickly hostility, and settled for that. The mid-ocean escorts were divided into groups and remained together, wherever possible, under one commander. Each group consisted, at full strength, of nine ships, usually three destroyers and six corvettes or frigates. In early 1943 there were 12 groups, seven British and five Canadian — an indication of the growing importance of Canada in the struggle. The Canadians were based at St. John's, Newfoundland, and the usual routine was for one of their groups to pick up a convoy off Newfoundland for escort to Britain, go into Londonderry for a brief rest, and then bring another convoy back; the British did the same thing in reverse. Canada also provided the Western Local Escort Force, which protected North Atlantic convoys from the "Western Ocean Meeting Point" off Newfoundland to the terminal ports of Sydney, Halifax, Boston and New York; the RCN used this force for the breaking-in of new ships and the training of crews on this now quiet coast before transferring them to the perilous mid-ocean routes.

These newly commissioned ships, with recently recruited crews, as well as veteran ships coming out of refit, had undergone operational training (similar to that at Tobermory) at St. Margaret's Bay, near Halifax. There a British submarine, *Seawolf*, as

186. HMCS *Loch Alvie* (frigate) shown alongside a surrendered U-boat. Frigates were faster and better-armed than corvettes.

185. The forecastle of HMCS *North Bay* (corvette) showing the "hedgehog" mounted.

well as a Dutch one, were used for "work-ups". Five or six ships, preparing for convoy duty, struggled with near-impossible demands that kept crews on their toes at all hours, day and night.

There was also a handful of escorts that were not members of escort groups but which could be formed into support groups — usually of six to eight ships — as required. As the name implies, they were directed to the support of any convoy under heavy U-boat attack. Mostly based in Iceland, they included five U.S. Coast Guard cutters, the largest warships taking part in convoy work. Support groups were very useful; they were able to fall back and patiently hunt the U-boats without creating a gap in the escort screen.

As for air support, one Coastal Command squadron operating from two locations — Northern Ireland and Iceland — had VLR (Very Long Range) Liberators; these had extra fuel tanks fitted in the bomb bays, which gave them an extreme range of about 2,300 miles. These aircraft could fly to the middle of the Atlantic and back from either base; the trouble was there were only a score of them, far too few to give continuous cover over the black pit.

187. A Canso of the RCAF, on patrol.

Not before March did a second Liberator squadron come into action. Two squadrons, based in the Outer Hebrides, had Flying Fortresses; their range could not match that of the Liberators, but they could take over the protection of convoys, once within range, freeing the Liberators for more distant work. Five squadrons (two of them Canadian) in Northern Ireland or in Scotland had Sunderlands — British flying boats with a range of 1,300 miles, slow and lumbering. All these squadrons were in 15 Group, RAF, Coastal Command. Two squadrons, one RAF with Hudsons and one USN with Catalinas, were based on Iceland; and in Newfoundland were three more — one U.S. with Fortresses and two RCAF flying Cansoes (the amphibian version of the Catalina) and Hudsons. Additional U.S. and Canadian squadrons covered American and Canadian coastal waters. Another group of Coastal Command patrolled between the Hebrides and Iceland, and a second the Bay of Biscay. The task of the first was to attack U-boats in transit between Germany and the North Atlantic killing-ground, the second those travelling to and from the main U-boat bases on the French coast. Their aircraft were a constant danger to U-boats and

188. Air patrols extended their range,

189. and were a constant threat to the U-boats.

scored steadily. But all were hampered by the bad winter weather.

This was the order of battle at the beginning of February 1943. On the 4th a convoy of 53 merchantmen, escorted by a British escort group of eight ships, had passed through Doenitz's patrol line on a pitch black night when snowflake, discharged accidentally, was spotted by one U-boat. Twenty-one boats converged on the convoy and others followed; a support group from Iceland arrived on the 5th, as did Liberators from their Iceland base. In the course of a three-day battle the combined strength of the escorting ships and aircraft held off the U-boats for the loss of only two stragglers, but, early on the 7th two escorts raced off to investigate a radar contact. U-boats broke through the gap this created; on that day and the next 13 ships were sunk, including an American troopship carrying men to Iceland. Two hundred soldiers and marines were lost — their bodies, supported by life-jackets, bobbing stiffly in the icy water. Three U-boats were destroyed, one by a Liberator that caught it as it crash-dived; seagulls were seen to dive for stunned fish — and for the

human remains that floated up from the shattered boat. Two more boats were damaged; and a further compensation was that Doenitz's preoccupation with this convoy — together with accurate intelligence concerning his moves — permitted two other convoys to get through safely. *B. Dienst* gave warning of the departure of another convoy at mid-month and the U-boats intercepted its 63 ships on the 21st. The battle lasted until the convoy reached the cover of the Newfoundland air patrols four days later. Eleven merchantmen went down (including six stragglers) for two U-boats sunk. Shipping losses for the month topped the 300,000-ton figure. Prospects for a German victory seemed bright, for Doenitz was well able to replace his boats. Such determined "pack" attacks, the Admiralty concluded, were bound to overwhelm a purely *surface* escort by sheer weight of numbers; increased long-range air support was direly needed. And the British War Cabinet received notice that the consumption of raw materials and military supplies was now exceeding imports; should the pattern continue for another two months the requirements of Allied strategy could no longer be met.

190. Attacks from the air mounted.

191. Aircraft scored steadily.

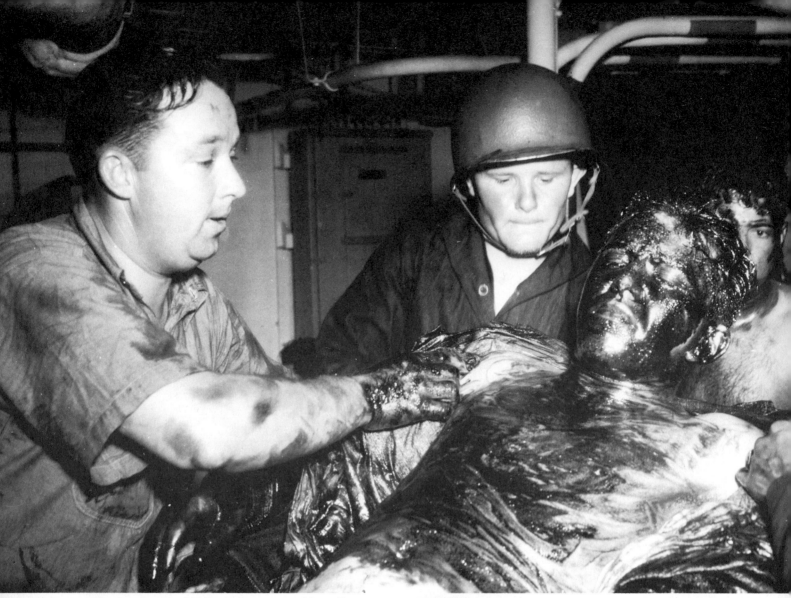

192. An oil-soaked U.S. marine, rescued from the sea.

Early in March the problem was discussed in Washington at a meeting of representatives of the British, Canadian and U.S. navies under the chairmanship of Admiral King. Air cover, it was stressed, was the only way to beat the U-boat packs, and only 23 VLR Liberators were in use. King controlled more than 100, but he had sent most of them to the Pacific theatre. Nor did he wish to recall them, suggesting, as an alternative, that Liberators be diverted from the bombing of Germany. An urgent appeal from Churchill to Roosevelt followed, and the President settled the matter. He sent a squadron of Liberators — not from the U.S. Navy but from the U.S. Army Air Force — to Newfoundland; but it was early April before they arrived.

Meanwhile a convoy battle that lasted from 7–10 March resulted in the loss of 13 ships for no U-boats sunk. In the first week of March — thanks to intelligence of the whereabouts of patrol lines derived from German messages — convoys had been successfully threaded through, but an

193. A tanker, ablaze and sinking. A column of flame, changing into thick black smoke, lights up the ocean.

194. A VLR Liberator provides air-cover for a convoy. Because of its long range, the aircraft could reach the formerly unprotected gap in mid-Atlantic.

intelligence blackout that began on 8 March hampered the British for a few days. On that day Doenitz had ordered the fourth rotor of the U-boat "enigma" machines to be activated and the millions of additional permutations had to be unravelled — a task that at first seemed hopeless, but which was successfully accomplished by the British "Bletchley Bombe" computers. During this period, when there was no knowledge of the U-boat dispositions, another convoy — accompanied by an escort carrier and a strong escort group — was mauled in a battle that lasted from 10—12 March: one destroyer and four merchantmen were sunk; two U-boats were accounted for. These battles were mostly fought at night, the last in squalls of snow, and were ghastly, especially for ships carrying oil or ammunition. Gusts of flame engulfed the tankers in seconds after the torpedoes struck; munitions ships simply blew apart in a roar of flame and smoke. One U-boat commander, in his log,

described steel plates and other metal, hurled hundreds of feet into the air, clanging down on his metal deck as the boat knifed through the convoy lines. The while crests of waves and driving snow took on an orange cast in the lurid light that at times was as bright as daylight.

A westbound convoy, sighted by the Germans on 13 March, got through safely after Huff-Duff picked up the sighting signal. An escort drew the wolf pack after her while the convoy swung away. The next convoys, HX229 and SC122, about which a whole book has been written,* were not so fortunate.

These convoys together contained 88 merchant ships. Though British decrypting was back on stream, *B. Dienst* on this occasion decrypted British messages in time for Doenitz to make use of them. He was able to move his boats across the track of newly-ordered diversions that should have pulled the convoys clear. A U-boat sighted HX229 early on 16 March and shadowed it during the day. The

Convoy, by Martin Middlebrook

pack attacked on a night that was bright with moonlight; four ships were sunk. Rescue operations, and a fruitless asdic search, left the convoy with only two escorts. Though a support group was ordered to the scene from Iceland to reinforce the defence, the convoy's immediate prospects were far from rosy.

The wisdom of leaving escorts behind for rescue work may be questioned, and a cold-blooded decision not to do so may be long debated. In this case the escort commander faced the terrible choice between leaving men (and some women and children who were passengers) to almost certain death, and his duty — which was to protect the ships that remained in his convoy. Compassion determined the course he took.

Meanwhile, early on the 17th, SC122 was sighted. The sighting U-boat sank two freighters, set a third on fire and crippled a fourth in a sudden, surprise attack. Both convoys, surrounded by U-boats, faced a day-long assault. Two ships from HX229 went down, but as the U-boats closed in on SC122 a VLR Liberator from Northern Ireland suddenly reached the scene. The astonished U-boat

commanders, with the taste of victory already in their mouths, found themselves forced to dive to escape attack. The time the aircraft could take over the convoy was limited, however, and it soon turned away for its base. The U-boats surfaced and had sunk a freighter when the arrival of a second Liberator forced them down again. HX229, a hundred miles astern, lost four more ships when, in the afternoon, a Liberator reached that convoy also. It circled for four hours, causing the submarines to discontinue their attacks.

The battle continued throughout the 18th, and in all, though the unexpected air cover had deprived Doenitz of the annihilating victory he had expected, the convoys lost 22 ships (145,500 tons) with cargoes amounting to 161,000 tons. Three new Liberty ships were among them. Only one U-boat, depth-charged from the air, was sunk (19 March) when the battle was virtually over. The battle was also costly for the Allies in human terms: 360 people (including two women and two children) lost their lives.

This brought losses during the first 20 days of March to 97 ships (more than 500,000 tons) — almost all of them from heavily-defended convoys. This rate of sinkings was *twice* the rate of new

195. Liberators at Aldergrove, Northern Ireland, a well-situated field for convoy protection.

1943

196. A U-boat, depth-charged from the air.

tonnage being constructed, even in 1943. In the same period the Germans lost only seven U-boats, less than *half* the new boats coming into service. One of them, *U-87*, was shared by HMC Ships *St. Croix* and *Shediac* (corvette). Well might the Admiralty state that "the Germans never came so near to disrupting communications between the New World and the Old as in the first twenty days of March, 1943". And yet the air gap, which was responsible for the heavy losses, could have been covered. A Liberator had reached the furthermost convoy, HX229, from Northern Ireland (some 1,000 miles), whereas Newfoundland, where there were as yet no Liberators, had been only 840 miles from the ships.

Towards the end of March another three convoys were at sea, and Doenitz rallied his boats for another mass attack. Three things helped the Allies — hurricane-force gales, which hampered the U-boats more than the escorts; the provision of an

197. HMCS *Shediac* (corvette).

escort carrier, USS *Bogue*, which sailed with the only convoy to be attacked; and the precision of British intelligence. Because of the latter, the disposition of the U-boats was known; it was

198. USS *Bogue* (escort carrier).

199. Rear-Admiral L.W. Murray, RCN.

possible to switch a support group from one convoy to the next to "punch a hole" through U-boat patrol lines. (Additional ships, from the support group, travelled ahead and on the bows of the merchant ships. They protected the convoy from the line of U-boats, lying in wait ahead). Once through the line, *Bogue* flew its Avengers and Wildcats to keep the U-boats down while the convoy plodded on its way. Much to the relief of the Admiralty, only one ship was lost from these convoys.

Allied fortunes, which seemed to turn with these three convoys, continued to rise in April. That month Liberators, equipped with centimetric radar, began to operate from Newfoundland; support groups contained more escort carriers; CAM-ships, with three or four Swordfish aircraft, were often with the convoys. And a redistribution of responsibilities for Atlantic warfare — which had been agreed at the Washington naval conference in March by Britain, Canada and the United States, and which made for much greater efficiency — came into effect. It had been mutually agreed that Britain and Canada, whose provision of escorts now was roughly equal, should share complete responsibility for the vital northern routes. This freed Canada from U.S. control, which had irked her, and gave her operational charge of convoys west of the CHOP line (Change of Operational Control Line) based on the 47° West meridian; east of that Britain, through Admiral Sir Max Horton,

C.-in C. Western Approaches, had control. Canada appointed Rear-Admiral L.W. Murray (as Commander-in-Chief Canadian Northwest Atlantic) to exercise these new responsibilities and Newfoundland became a sub-command.

Leonard Murray was born and raised in Nova Scotia. He was a member of the first graduating class from the Royal Naval College of Canada, established in 1911. There was no scope for young naval officers in Canada at that time and at 17 he was sent for experience to the Royal Navy. He served with the British throughout the First World War and gained first-hand experience of convoy work. By the time the Second World War came he was Deputy Chief of the Naval Staff in Ottawa. A specialist in navigation, an advocate of the corvette and an experienced convoy-man, Murray was a "sailor's sailor" and the right man for the job.

The change illustrated most dramatically the stature that the Royal Canadian Navy had by now acquired. The Americans had sole responsibility for the New York–Gibraltar convoys; the Trinidad–Great Britain oil convoys; and the whole of the western South Atlantic where, with "hunter-killer" groups (the equivalent of support groups), they were to make a magnificent contribution in the war against the U-boats. Each of these co-equal commands ran its own show and used its own procedures.

April passed in ding-dong fashion but it was obvious, as the month wore on, that antidotes — so carefully built up in the preceding years — were beginning to come together and to be, at last, effective. Liberators closed the air gap, so that U-boats found themselves under attack in areas they had assumed no land-based aircraft could reach; centimetric radar pinpointed targets with clarity and with accuracy. Huff-Duff directed the escorts to the U-boats, whose radio chatter was like the yelping of wolves, with great precision. Aircraft from escort carriers and CAM-ships forced the U-boats down, spoiling their attacks. Support groups began to arrive in time to turn the tide of battle and the new hedgehog multiple mortar claimed its first victim in a battle that began at the end of April. In April 344,680 tons of shipping were lost world-wide, less than half the figure for March. The tonnage lost to U-boats was more than compensated for by new construction; and the rise in U-boat losses — the 15 sunk in April doubled the March figure — was gratifying for the Allies.

The decisive battle of the Atlantic war began on 28 April when a convoy (ONS-5) of 42 ships, escorted by a destroyer, a frigate and four corvettes, entered the danger zone. Doenitz had organized three groups of U-boats to receive it. It was a propitious time, for the Iceland air patrols were unable to fly because of bad weather. Nevertheless the surface escorts beat off five attacks, until early on the 29th when a U-boat sank a freighter. Three escorts, unable to refuel in heavy seas, left for Newfoundland to pick up oil, but five destroyers from a support group replaced them. The attackers, reinforced by Doenitz, numbered 40 boats. Nevertheless an aggressive defence, running out on Huff-Duff and radar fixes, kept the U-boats down. Not until 4 May did heavy pressure finally break the screen; five ships, torpedoed against the northern lights, sank quickly. Intelligence, warned of the U-boat strength, ordered another support group to

200. The range of escorts could be extended by refuelling at sea. Here the fuel line is being brought in from a tanker.

the scene. RCAF aircraft from Newfoundland, despite bad weather, appeared to keep the U-boats under. A heavy storm both hindered and helped the convoy. It hampered the U-boats, but it caused the convoy to straggle, the stragglers, deprived of defence, being picked off one by one.

Throughout the 5th the U-boats kept up the pressure, torpedoing two ships in the convoy. With night, Doenitz signalled, "the drumroll . . . must begin". Fog came down and, as the U-boats closed in for the kill, radar gave the escorts a distinct advantage; only one submarine got through the defences, to sink two freighters, while, in a short space of time five U-boats were sunk. When Doenitz called off the battle — for if the U-boats lingered they would face increasing air attack from Newfoundland — he had lost seven U-boats; five more suffered severe and another 12 lesser damage. The Allies had lost 12 ships. The lesson was now clear; if U-boats, no matter what their number,

1943

tackled well-defended convoys, they could expect to suffer losses that were unacceptable.

Doenitz, with some 130 boats in the North Atlantic alone in May — the highest number so far — refused to recognize it until the Allies forced the lesson home. Morale in the U-boat crews was declining. Commanders who had become experienced when Allied defences were weak had nevertheless gone to the bottom one by one; they were replaced by raw commanders who, faced with experienced anti-submarine tactics and advanced technology, especially from the air, succumbed more quickly. HMCS *Drumheller* (corvette), a British frigate, (HMS *Lagan*) and an aircraft from No. 423 Squadron, RCAF, for example, co-operated in perfect fashion to share the sinking of *U-456*. Doenitz was to lose 41 boats in May (including one commanded by his son), and this was a price he could no longer afford to pay. On the 24th an incredulous British intelligence team decrypted Doenitz's message to his U-boats, ordering them to withdraw from the North Atlantic. It was unexpected — almost too much to hope for — but Doenitz in his memoirs admitted that in May he knew that the Atlantic battle could no longer be won.

It was heavily-armed aircraft, flying in maritime patrols from the eastern seaboard or from Coastal Command's bases in Britain and Iceland, that eventually turned the tables. Though surface escorts had a long start (aircraft did not become fully effective until the black pit was closed in the spring of 1943), Canadian aircraft accounted for 21 U-boats against a total of 29 scored by Canadian naval ships through the whole war.

Eastern Air Command, RCAF, operated from bases that increased in number as the war progressed. Eventually they curved from Labrador through Newfoundland to the Maritimes. It was not until May 1941, however, that a U-boat entered its patrol area. The submarine was detected by direction-finding stations on the 21st, but aircraft despatched to the area could not find it. No fewer than 11 squadrons were operational in Eastern Air Command at the end of 1943; of them No. 10, proudly nicknamed the "North Atlantic Squadron", sank three U-boats.

The real measure of a tonnage war, such as the Battle of the Atlantic, is not expressed, however, merely in terms of U-boats sunk. It is to be found in the number of merchant ships, bearing precious cargoes, that get through. If the attacks of U-boats

201. HMCS *Kootenay* (destroyer) sends a pattern of "hedgehog" bombs into the Bay of Biscay in August 1944. *U-621* sank as the result of this attack, which *Kootenay* shared with two other Canadian destroyers, *Ottawa* (background) and *Chaudiere*.

202. HMCS *Drumheller* (corvette).

— no matter how many boats the enemy has — can be spoiled, either by surface escorts or by aircraft, the battle is won. The full measure of the air contribution can be found in the thousands upon thousands of hours flown through weather that was often bad, carefully searching the vast expanse of water, forcing the enemy to go down and to stay submerged while the convoys ploughed on, unmolested.

203. "This was a price he could no longer afford to pay."

204. "The strain of searching waters for hours on end. . . . ." A Hudson of No. 11 (Bomber Reconnaissance) Squadron, RCAF.

The men who flew with the Altantic squadrons came, in the main, from Britain, Canada, Australia and New Zealand. They were chosen — especially pilots and navigators — from those who had topped their training courses. Navigators, in particular, had to be greatly skilled if they were to find convoys a thousand miles out in the trackless wastes and then, fifteen hours or so after takeoff — and dead weary — to make a precise landfall to bring their comrades safely home. The greatest enemies of these crews were strain and boredom. The strain of searching waters for hours on end to spot the low shape of a submarine or the tiny wake of a periscope; and the boredom of isolated bases on both sides of the Atlantic and in Iceland, as well as the staleness of long flights with little to see save clouds and the moody Atlantic Ocean. The record

of 423 Squadron, RCAF, gives the story:

Operational flying hours: 16,277. Victories, U-boat: 3 sunk, 2 shared, 1 damaged. Delivered 201 depth-charges in 26 attacks. Casualties (operational), 6 aircraft, 43 aircrew of whom 40 were killed or presumed dead, two wounded, one injured in a flying accident.

Aircrews of this squadron flew more than 16,000 hours; they attacked only 26 times — sinking, helping to sink, or damaging six U-boats and being shot down themselves. This gives an average of 615 hours flying for each attack and well over 2,600 hours for each success!

It was the dedication of such men, who realized that the cause was bigger than themselves — as well as that of naval and merchant seamen — that brought a decisive end to the grim Battle of the Atlantic.

Doenitz did not give up easily nevertheless;

205. Few members of U-boat crews survived. Here are
some who did.

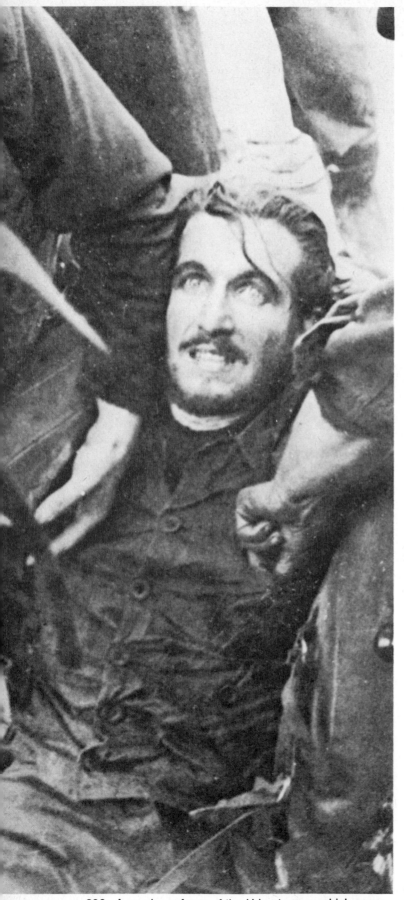

206. A survivor of one of the U-boat crews which were "hunted, pounced upon and driven."

though the Battle of the Atlantic may have been won, it was not yet over and it was imperative, on the part of the escorts and supporting aircraft, to keep the initiative. Escorts were becoming plentiful. Canada got four more destroyers (ex-British) that summer, which she named *Kootenay*, *Gatineau*, *Saskatchewan* and *Ottawa* (replacing *Ottawa* sunk in 1942). In September Canada's first "home-built" destroyer *Micmac* (Tribal Class) was launched. Doenitz still had over 400 U-boats. He concentrated, during June, July and August, on the Azores, for which he had to use the Bay of Biscay area where German fighters and bombers, fitted with new radio-controlled glider bombs, could give support. The Allies, therefore, hunted in the Bay. The Canadian corvettes *Edmundston*, *Calgary* and *Snowberry*, though heavily attacked from the air, escaped being sunk; HMCS *Athabaskan*, however, was severely damaged. Two of these corvettes, with a British frigate, shared the sinking of *U-536* in November. After changing their codes at the end of May, the British had the upper hand in the intelligence war, for Doenitz's orders to his U-boats betrayed his intentions. Twenty-five U-boats were sunk in Coastal Command's "Bay Offensive" and another 49 on the northern transit routes and other areas for a loss of only 58 merchant ships. The score was disastrous from Doenitz's point of view, and the experience for U-boat crews, as British Intelligence put it, one "of being hunted, pounced upon and driven to an extent and with a continuity which human flesh and blood, inspired by no national victories, cannot possibly be expected to endure".

Doenitz did, however, expect his U-boat commanders "to endure". The Allies, as had been decided at Casablanca, had invaded Sicily successfully in July and the enormous convoys required had steamed from American and British ports with minor loss (three merchant ships lost from the "Slow Assault Convoy", torpedoed in the Mediterranean by Axis submarines, were carrying Canadian troops and transport; 58 Canadians lost their lives, and cargoes including 500 vehicles and 40 guns went to the bottom). Four Canadian landing craft flotillas had taken part in this invasion, as they were to do in the invasion of the Italian mainland, which followed early in September. The Allies had thus carried the war to Europe and, from the time of the conquest of Sicily, had freed the Mediterranean for merchant shipping. Useful as this was, it was not the vital theatre; it was an invasion of Northwest Europe that the Nazis feared most, and Doenitz appreciated that the Allied ability to mount an offensive there depended on the shipping to Britain of a continuous supply of men, munitions and equipment from the Western Hemisphere. It was his duty to cut those supply lines and, as he stated in his

1943

207. Canadian troops come ashore from landing craft at Reggio di Calabria, Italy, 3 September, 1943.

memoirs, "we had no option but to fight on". He would give his men new weapons to enable them to renew the battle. Submarines better than any the Germans then had in operation were being built.

With increased anti-aircraft armament, better search receivers (to give warning of the radar probes of hostile aircraft) and new acoustic torpedoes, Doenitz returned his U-boats to the North Atlantic lanes in September. The torpedoes, attracted by noise, homed on a ship's propellers. The boats set up the usual patrol lines from which they hoped to mount surprise attacks — which would now be aimed primarily at the escort vessels, not the merchant ships. Intelligence, well aware of the nature of the operation, enabled a support group and extra aircraft to be rapidly diverted to the area southwest of Iceland where the first battle developed.

Three escorts and six merchant ships were sunk by the U-boats, and one escort damaged. The first escort to be struck by the new and deadly weapon was the Canadian destroyer *St. Croix*; then a British corvette, *Polyanthus*, coming to her aid, was also sunk. A British ship, HMS *Itchen*, was able to pick up 81 of *St. Croix*'s crew, but later *Itchen* herself was struck and roared into flame. Only one member of *St. Croix*'s crew survived, and two from *Itchen*'s. It had not been one-sided, however, despite the new torpedo. The Germans lost three

208. HMCS *Magog* (frigate), listless in the waters off Newfoundland, the victim of an acoustic torpedo, 14 October, 1944.

209. A "Squid" being loaded.

U-boats; six were damaged. One of the U-boats was the victim of a new aerial acoustic torpedo, developed by the British.

In October the Azores were occupied (under arrangement with Portugal, Britain's oldest ally) and that closed the air gap still more firmly; continuous air cover could now be given in the whole of the North Atlantic. Surface escort groups were sufficient for every convoy and they were used by now to working together; radar, Huff-Duff and new weapons like the hedgehog, had nullified the U-boats' old advantages. (And by this time the "Squid", more efficient than the hedgehog, was coming in; this was a three-barrelled mortar that hurled projectiles containing 100 pounds of explosive ahead or abeam. Armed automatically in conjunction with an asdic-transmitter, its depth-ranging system was accurate.) An antidote to acoustic torpedoes had been found in the "Foxer" (British) and the "CAAT" (Canadian), noise-making devices that were towed astern of each ship to attract torpedoes. Support groups quickly reinforced threatened convoys and these were free to hunt, for hours if necessary, any U-boat that had submerged. Escort carriers could be provided for convoys, and VLR Liberators, long awaited, at last covered the ships. British intelligence knew the German moves and could divert convoys accordingly; *B. Dienst*, completely in the dark, could no longer frustrate those diversions by a timely switch of patrol lines. Indeed, by November, Doenitz found it hard to find any convoys at all; he was forced to scatter U-boats individually across the broad Atlantic wastes — an acknowledgment that wolf pack tactics, which had served him so well, had failed. Interceptions were made; ships were sunk. But from the end of 1943 the Americans, the British and the Canadians were masters in their respective zones.

210. Escort carriers in heavy seas.

The end of Hitler's navy

We may anticipate the end of the story. The confidence that the sea and air escorts had gained in their ability to drive off attacks never wavered until the war was over, despite Doenitz's growing reliance on reconnaissance aircraft to find his targets and his introduction, in the first months of 1944, of the "Schnorkel" submarine. The schnorkel, a long tube that could be raised like a periscope to suck in air, enabled the submarine to run at schnorkel-depth on its diesels, and this prolonged the useful life of Type VII and Type IX U-boats until the end of the war. This device, in fact, converted what were really fast, submersible torpedo-boats into true submarines — vessels able to escape radar surveillance and air attacks by operating underwater. Though a continuing problem for Coastal Command, they were slow when submerged and had been introduced too late to affect the outcome in the North Atlantic. At this time, in any case, Doenitz was becoming more and more preoccupied with the Allied invasion of Northwest Europe — anywhere from Norway to the South of France — which was obviously imminent.

The new, high-performance submarines that Doenitz had projected in 1943 (Type XVII's and Type XVIII's — later modified to the 1,600-ton Type XXI, which could achieve a submerged speed faster than almost any escort) had suffered from teething troubles, which were, in the main, difficulties with steel and labour. Using his new relationship with Hitler, Doenitz overcame them. Nevertheless, with conventional construction methods, the fleet would not be ready before 1946. Albert Speer (Armaments Minister) cut that to the spring of 1944 by using mass production and prefabrication techniques (much as the American Liberty ships were built). Eight hull units would be built separately, inland, and shipped by canals to

211. The schnorkel above the water.

212. The schnorkel device fitted the horizontal tube
shown here at the side of the U-boat's conning tower.

213. A Type XXI U-boat. The compact, squat conning
tower gave a minimum of drag and that, combined
with powerful motors, provided speed.

The End of Hitler's Navy

214. The interior of a U-boat pen. The roof, of reinforced
concrete, was 5.5 metres thick.

ports for final assembly. The programme was severely disrupted by Allied bombing; even canals, whose banks were breached, ran dry. And in August 1944, 617 (''Dambuster'') Squadron, RAF, put its new ''Tallboy'' bombs through the roofs of the concrete U-boat shelters. It was not until April 1945 that *U-2511*, the first Type XXI, emerged into the Atlantic, where it was picked up on asdic; racing away from the escort at a *submerged* speed of 18 knots, the submarine easily outpaced its pursuer. The boat was off Panama awaiting victims when, on 4 May, just prior to the surrender, it received Doenitz's signal to return to base. The weapon with which the Germans had hoped to regain the initiative in the North Atlantic had come far too late.

In fact it was the Allies who took the offensive in the first half of 1944, both by air and by sea. ''Fortress Europe'' was bombed, largely to destroy communications and reduce the German ability to interfere with the projected invasion of Normandy from the air. Before D-Day the Allies struck at the enemy's warships, U-boats and merchant ships all along the Atlantic coast. Canadian ships and two Motor Torpedo Boat flotillas recently formed by Canada took part. In one of these operations off the Brittany coast the destroyers *Haida*, *Athabaskan* and *Huron* surprised three German destroyers. *Athabaskan* and *Haida*, regardless of risk, pursued one through a British minefield and set it ablaze, and *Haida* sank it. Two days later (April 28) *Haida* and *Athabaskan* had encountered two more destroyers, when *Athabaskan* — torpedoed — sank. *Haida* continued the fight, driving one of the destroyers, blazing and heavily damaged by gunfire, onto the beach.

The captain of *Haida*, Commander Harry De Wolf (who was to become Vice-Admiral and a Chief of the Naval Staff), then steamed to the aid of the stricken *Athabaskan*. When he arrived there was no trace of the destroyer, but dark groups of survivors could be seen in the water. He stopped *Haida*'s engines and the ship glided in to where the clusters of men were thickest. De Wolf knew that his first responsibility was the safety of his ship; the stationary *Haida* was a sitting duck, close to the enemy coast and an easy mark for air attack. Nevertheless he made up his mind to wait for fifteen minutes, to lower a whaler and to haul in as many survivors as he could. His men pulled and pushed exhausted members of *Athabaskan*'s crew, filthy

216. Harry De Wolf, when Lt.-Cdr., is shown at the left with Lt.-Cdr. H.N. Lay (then commanding *Restigouche*) and Lt.-Cdr. J.C. Hibbard (*Skeena*).

with oil, into the whaler and up the scramble nets. The fifteen minutes elapsed and still De Wolf lingered. Finally a voice from a nearby raft, believed to be that of Lieutenant-Commander John Stubbs, *Athabaskan*'s young captain, was heard calling, ''Get away, *Haida*, get clear!'' Reluctantly De Wolf ordered ''slow ahead''. In all, *Haida* saved 44 of *Athabaskan*'s crew; 83 were picked up by the Germans and became prisoners-of-war; Stubbs, and 128 men, were lost.

The fight, a minor classic, had been pressed with skill and determination by the Canadian ships, and two for one is not a bad score.

In Coastal Command, RAF, three of 40 anti-submarine squadrons were Canadian. Two of the seven squadrons used for air strikes against enemy shipping off the north coast of Scotland, in the North Sea, the English Channel and the Bay of Biscay were also Canadian. In all, seven RCAF squadrons* served at one time or another in Coastal Command. No. 162 Squadron was transferred from Newfoundland to Iceland in January 1944 and began to operate its Cansoes from there. The squadron was most successful against U-boats that were desperately trying to move from Norway to counteract the Allied forces when the invasion came in June. The squadron had already sunk one U-boat

215. U-boat pens at Lorient, on the Bay of Biscay, are shown here under aerial bombardment. Not until the ''Tallboy'' bomb, invented by Barnes Wallis of Britain, came into use in 1944 could the pens be pierced. By that time the Battle of the Atlantic had been won at sea.

*One of them (No. 413) had an interesting history; it operated over the North Sea late in 1941 but with Japan's entry into the war moved to Ceylon early in 1942 and patrolled, in the main, over the Indian Ocean. A Catalina of this squadron gave warning of the approach of a Japanese fleet to Ceylon; the island's defences were alerted and the Japanese attack repulsed.

The End of Hitler's Navy

217. Beaufighters, using rockets and cannon-fire, attack a German ship off the coast of France.

in April; in June it sank five out of six sighted. On 24 June Flight-Lieutenant David E. Hornell of this squadron won the Victoria Cross. Sighting a U-boat, Hornell flew towards it. The U-boat remained on the surface and opened anti-aircraft fire at a range of about 1,000 yards just as the Canso was positioning for attack. The starboard engine, hit, caught fire and set the whole wing blazing — stripping the surface so that only the ribs remained. The Canadian, with superhuman effort, altered course to match the U-boat's sudden turn and straddled it with depth charges. It went to the bottom.

Hornell, whose starboard engine had now dropped off, was forced to ditch into 12-foot waves. The Canso bounced twice from crests (the first time more than 100 feet) but on the third attempt he managed to get down smoothly — difficult enough to accomplish even with a sound aircraft in light seas. His crew escaped, but a dinghy burst through over-inflation, leaving one five-man type to be

shared by eight. The survivors were afloat for 21 hours before being rescued — taking turns in the water to cut down weight. Two men died. Hornell himself sank into a coma and could not be revived.

Canadian squadrons made up about 9 per cent of Coastal Command's total force; in addition, almost one-fifth of the aircrew of RAF units in Coastal Command were Canadians. One of them, Flying Officer K.O. Moore, sank two U-boats in 20 minutes early on 8 June 1944 — a feat unequalled in the Second World War. Coastal Command sank 178 U-boats; 16 of these were sunk by Canadian squadrons, a score roughly proportionate to strength. And of 110 submarines damaged, the RCAF had 10 — again a figure in accordance with squadron strength. Aircraft of Canada's Eastern Air Command accounted for six U-boats sunk and three damaged.

As a result of these and British operations, a vast armada put an Allied invading force and its supplies safely ashore in Normandy on D-Day (6 June 1944) without interference from German aircraft or U-boats. The naval task, "in conjunction with the

218. Coastal Command aircraft sink German U-boats.

219. RAF air-sea rescue launch approaches Hornell's dinghy.

220. Coastal Command accounted for 178 U-boats.

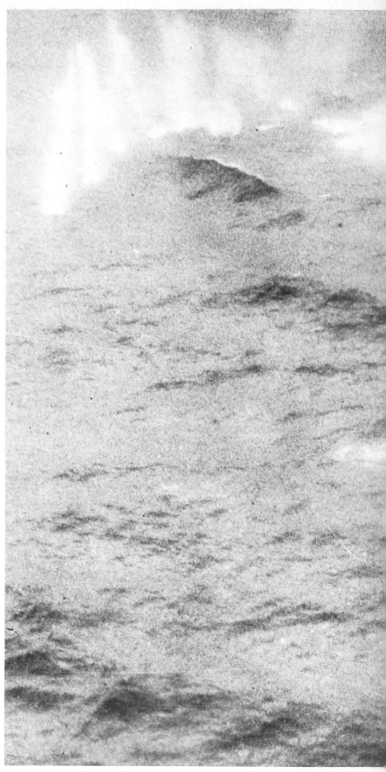

221. Another Coastal Command attack.

Merchant Navies of the United Nations, and supported by the Allied Air Forces, to carry the Allied Expeditionary Force to the Continent, to establish it there in a secure bridgehead and to build it up and maintain it at a rate that will outmatch that of the enemy'', was fulfilled. The tally of shipping to do all this was enormous: six battleships, two monitors, 32 cruisers, 93 destroyers, 15 sloops, 26

The End of Hitler's Navy

escort destroyers, 27 frigates, 71 corvettes and scores of smaller naval craft. There were hundreds of landing ships and landing craft to carry the troops and guns and tanks with which to assault the beaches. The total number of ships and vessels used in all phases of the invasion — the assault, follow-up, build-up and administration — was 7,016. D-Day was the triumphant climax to nearly five years of bitter warfare in the North Atlantic.

Canada had provided part of the vast invasion fleet. *Prince Henry* and *Prince David*, converted from armed merchant cruisers to landing ships, infantry, were included, having with them two Canadian landing craft flotillas. Three others (with large craft capable of crossing the Channel under their own power) also took part. Three Canadian destroyers (*Huron, Iroquois* and *Haida*) were there, as well as several escort groups made up of

222. A Canadian "Bangor Class" minesweeper has swept and marked a safe channel for D-Day invasion ships, which are viewed from the minesweeper's stern.

223. Part of the invasion fleet, covered by barrage balloons to prevent dive-bombing, crosses the Channel. RCN landing craft are shown here.

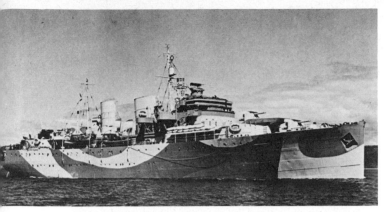

224. HMCS *Prince Henry*, converted to an infantry landing ship, took part in the invasion of Normandy

225. — as did HMCS *Prince David*.

Canadian destroyers, frigates and corvettes; two destroyers (*Algonquin* and *Sioux*) were part of the bombarding force. Both Motor Torpedo Boat flotillas participated. Six Canadian ("Bangor") minesweepers helped sweep mines from the path of the invading fleets in the British sector; 10 others (the Canadian 31st Minesweeping Flotilla) swept the way to an American beach ("Omaha"). This main invasion was followed, in August, by an invasion of southern France; again *Prince David* and *Prince Henry* helped carry the invading force.

The invasion of Northwest Europe forced the Germans to fight on three fronts. By the end of the year the Allies had freed France and Belgium and advanced into Holland; in the south they had cleared most of Italy and were close to Bologna; and the Russians, who had been sustained by Allied supplies when their defeat seemed certain, were rolling irresistibly from the east towards the frontier of Germany itself. In March 1945, having crossed the Rhine, the Allies drove deep into German territory; on 25 April U.S. and Russian forces met on the Elbe, cutting the German defending forces in two. Five days later Hitler shot himself as the Russians cleared Berlin. "Victory in Europe" was celebrated on 8 May, by which time the Germans had capitulated.

The fortunes of the Battle of the Atlantic, which was just as decisive for survival (and ultimate victory) as the Battle of Britain, had run in the Germans' favour for more than three years. In March 1943 they practically had it won. The following month the balance swung once and for all

226. Here the assault landing craft, carrying Canadian troops, leave *Prince David*.

227. HMCS *Clayoquot* (Bangor class minesweeper).

in the Allies' favour. And that, a vital prerequisite, meant that D-Day — in June 1944 — could take place to spell the fate of Hitler's Reich. In the year before D-Day, for example, U-boats sank only 92 ships out of the thousands that were delivering the men and supplies that would bring about the ultimate defeat of Germany. There were plenty of escorts for slow, patient hunts. In the first three months Canadian ships either sank, or co-operated in the sinking of, many U-boats: HMCS *Camrose* — *U-757; Waskesiu — U-257; Prince Rupert — U-575; Swansea — U-448; St. Laurent, Owen Sound and Swansea — U-845. Waskesiu*, the first frigate to be built in a Canadian shipyard for the RCN, was, perhaps appropriately, the first frigate to score a kill. In March 1944 *U-744* was hunted for 32 hours by no less than seven escorts, five of them Canadian, before the boat was at last forced to the surface. HMCS *Chilliwack*(corvette) did get a boarding party alongside, but the seacocks had been opened and the submarine sank. As late as April, however, a U-boat torpedoed HMCS *Valleyfield* (frigate) off Newfoundland, sending her to the bottom with 125 of her company. The ship split in two and sank rapidly.

228. Boarding party from HMCS *Chilliwack* (corvette) alongside *U-744*.

The End of Hitler's Navy

229. A British X-craft (midget submarine).

230. The escort carrier *Nabob* lists to starboard after being hit by a torpedo off the coast of Norway.

It had been costly for both sides. After April 1943, 590 U-boats were destroyed (only 194 had been accounted for in the previous 3½years), 290 of them by aircraft alone, 174 by ships alone, and the remainder (save a few from other causes) by a combination of ships and aircraft. Of 39,000 members of U-boat crews throughout the war, 28,000 lost their lives and 5,000 became prisoners of war. Figures for Allied merchant ships and merchant seamen are less precise (because of the many Allied and neutral nations involved), but it is certain that more than 5,000 ships were lost in all, and that almost 3,000 of them were sunk by U-boats; additionally, the U-boats sank 148 Allied warships, including three aircraft carriers and two battleships. More than 50,000 Allied merchant seamen (and they bore the brunt, with little hope of

advancement and for the ''going'' rates of pay) gave up their lives; perhaps two-thirds of them were the victims of U-boats.

These were fearful losses in terms of human life — if we exclude the First World War, more than the combined deaths incurred in all the naval battles during the previous 500 years — and they are an indication of the severity of the Atlantic struggle.

— — — — —

It remains only to describe the fate of the heavy warships, which Doenitz had managed to retain and the majority of which we last met in Norwegian waters. During the night of 21–22 September 1943, four British ''midget'' (X-craft) submarines entered the Alten Fjord where *Tirpitz*, cocooned in anti-torpedo nets and guarded by anti-submarine

231. HMS *Duke of York* (battleship).

The End of Hitler's Navy

booms, lay silhouetted against the still-bright northern sky. Two penetrated the defences and planted mines under her hull. The damage immobilized the mighty battleship for six months. In another attack, by the Fleet Air Arm in August 1944, the Canadian-manned escort carrier *Nabob** was hit by acoustic torpedoes from a U-boat; severely damaged, she still made the 1,100-mile voyage home. Only the 31,000-ton battle-cruiser *Scharnhorst*, which had been transferred to Norway and was now lying in a branch of the Alten Fjord, remained with *Lützow* to pose a major threat to the Arctic convoys. *Lützow* left shortly afterwards for a refit in Germany. By the autumn of 1943 the greatest tank battle of the war — Kursk — had been fought and lost by the Germans in Russia and the Germans faced disaster. It is against this background that *Scharnhorst*, in a bid to cut deliveries of tanks and other equipment, ventured out late in December to tackle a Murmansk-bound convoy. Decrypted German signals pointed to their interest in the convoy, and it was known that a sortie by *Scharnhorst* was imminent. The British prepared accordingly. Crippled by the guns of the battleship HMS *Duke of York*, firing at long-range in almost total Arctic darkness, *Scharnhorst* was sent to the bottom on New Year's Day, 1944. Of 1,968 men aboard, only 36 were rescued. Some of those in the icy water managed to climb onto rafts and it was reported that they were singing "*Auf einem Seemansgrab, da blühen keine Rosen*" ("On a sailor's grave no roses bloom") — certainly no roses bloomed over the squally winter sea that was the grave of nearly all their shipmates.

Tirpitz, which after repairs had moved to Tromsö Fjord, succumbed to five-ton bombs delivered by the RAF. She capsized and foundered on 12 November 1944, taking 900 seamen with her. Of the remaining ships, *Gneisenau* never saw service again after being bombed in February 1943, as we have noted; she was scuttled off Gotenhafen, in the Baltic, as the Russians approached in March 1945. *Hipper*, *Admiral Scheer* and *Lützow* were destroyed from the air in April 1945, the first two at Kiel and *Lützow* off Swinemünde. *Leipzig*, rammed by *Prinz Eugen* near Danzig towards the end of 1944, and put out of service, was finally scuttled in the North Sea by the Allies in 1946. *Prinz Eugen*, the last of the big ships, surrendered to the Allies at Copenhagen in May 1945.

It was the end of Hitler's navy.

---

* *Nabob*'s aircraft. (*Puncher* was the second carrier manned by Canada).

Conclusion

Could the Battle of the Atlantic have been won without the help of Canada? Such questions, and the myriad imponderables that they raise, can never be clearly answered. It is said that if Napoleon had not had fried onions for supper on the night before Waterloo he would have won the battle; on the other hand, faced with other actions on Napoleon's part, Wellington might well have reacted differently. Without Canada, Britain *might* have let the Mediterranean go to put her main resources into the Atlantic struggle. And if, as a result, she had lost the oil from the Middle East, and the invasions of North Africa, Sicily and Italy had not been possible, could she have survived? A conclusive ending to the war in Europe depended on a step-by-step strategy (largely decided at Casablanca) that called for action in many theatres, as we have seen; the first and vital step was the winning of the Atlantic battle, and there is no doubt that, without Canada, the fight against the U-boats could not have been won in time. The Battle of the Atlantic, even with Canada's massive help, turned on a hair; and it was won with only just enough time to permit the massive build-up that was required for D-Day. And if D-Day had not taken place when it did — if it had been delayed only a couple of weeks — it could hardly have been launched in the teeth of the German "V" weapons that came into use shortly after D-Day. It was, therefore, a decisive struggle that was decided only just in time; and in it Canada played a decisive part.

232. The end of *Tirpitz* (Tromsö Fjord, 1944).

Suggested Further Reading

Canadian aspects

Appleton, T.E. *Usque Ad Mare*, Ottawa, Department of Transport, 1968. (Merchant ships)

Douglas, W.A.B. and Greenhous, Brereton *Out of the Shadows; Canada in the Second World War*, Toronto, Oxford University Press, 1977. (Contains a superficial "overview", sea and air)

Easton, Alan *50 North*, Toronto, Ryerson, 1963. (A first-class personal account of escort duty)

Goodspeed, D.J. (ed.) *The Armed Forces of Canada, 1867-1967*, Ottawa, Queen's Printer, 1967. (Contains good, brief histories of R.C.N. and Coastal Command participation)

Kostenuk, Sam and Griffin, John *RCAF: Squadron Histories and Aircraft, 1924-1968*, Toronto, Samuel Stevens, Hakkert, 1977. (Contains brief summaries of squadron activities, and illustrates types of aircraft used)

Lamb, James B. *The Corvette Navy*, Toronto, Macmillan, 1977. (An excellent, and humorous, personal narrative)

Macpherson, K.R. *Canada's Fighting Ships*, Toronto, Samuel Stevens, Hakkert, 1965. (Lists all participating ships, and illustrates each type)

Pugsley, W.H. *Sailor Remember*, Toronto, Collins, 1948. (A fine account of naval life, superbly illustrated)

Reader's Digest *The Canadians at War 1939/45* (Three vols.), Montreal, Reader's Digest, 1969. (Contains good personal accounts, and illustrates technology)

Roberts, Leslie *Canada's War at Sea*, vol. II, Montreal, A.H. Beatty, 1944. (Written while the war continued, it evokes the spirit of the time)

Schull, Joseph *The Far Distant Ships*, Ottawa, King's Printer, 1950. (Indispensable — the most comprehensive Canadian work)

Stacey, C.P. *Six Years of War*, Ottawa, Queen's Printer, 1966. (Covers the work of Canadian foresters and tunnellers in Britain)

Swettenham, John *McNaughton, 1939-1943*, vol. 2, Toronto, Ryerson, 1969.

Swettenham, John (ed.) *Valiant Men*, Toronto, Hakkert, 1973. (For further details on Victoria Cross winners)

Tucker, G.N. *The Naval Service of Canada*, vol. 2, Ottawa, King's Printer, 1952. (Covers RCN organization and shore establishments in great detail)

British aspects

Arnold-Foster, Mark *The World at War*, Glasgow, Collins, 1973. (Numerous "overall" histories of the Second World War suggest themselves; this one is recommended because of the way in which the significance of the Battle of the Atlantic is presented within the total framework)

Beesly, Patrick *Very Special Intelligence*, London, Hamish Hamilton, 1977. (The best book on wartime naval intelligence yet written)

Behrens, C.B.A. *Merchant Shipping and the Demands of War*, London, HMSO, 1955. (For those interested in the merchant navy's part, this is the standard work)

Hughes, Terry and Costello, John *The Battle of the Atlantic*, New York, Dial Press/James Wade, 1977. (An intensely readable account which says little, unfortunately, about Canadian participation)

Marwick, Arthur *The Home Front*, London, Thames & Hudson, 1976. (Good for the effects of the battle on food supplies, and on war material)

Monsarrat, Nicholas *The Cruel Sea*, London, Cassell, 1951. (Superb, for atmosphere)

Pawle, Gerald *Secret Weapons of World War II*, New York, Ballantine, 1967. (Describes technology in layman's terms)

Ranff, B.M. "U-boats; the tide turns", *History of the Second World War*, vol. 6, No. XI. London, Purnell, 1971.

Roskill, S.W. *The War at Sea*, vols. I-IV, London, HMSO, 1954-1961. (The best of the official histories, both British and Canadian)

Watts, Anthony *The U-boat Hunters*, London, Macdonald and Jane's, 1976. (An excellent account of anti-submarine warfare)

German aspects

Bekker, Cajus *Hitler's Naval War*, Garden City N.Y., Doubleday, 1974. (A comprehensive, "other side of the hill", account)

Rohwer, Jurgen *The Critical Convey Battles of March, 1943*, Annapolis, Naval Institute Press, 1977.

Political

Lowenheim, F.L., Langley, H.D. and Jones, Manfred (eds.) *Roosevelt and Churchill; their Secret Wartime Correspondence*, New York, Dutton, 1975.

Index of Naval Vessels

General Index

GREENLAND

CANADA

NEWFOUNDLAND

U501
CHAMBLY
MOOSEJAW

■ LEVIS

FAREWELL

U210
ASSINIBOINE

U588
SKEENA
WESTASKIWIN

U90
ST. CROIX

OTTAWA ■

U877
ST. THOMAS

CHARLOTTETOWN ■ ■ RACCOON

■ BRAS D'OR

CHEDABUCTO ■

SHAWINIGAN ■

St John's

Placentia Bay

CAPE RACE

■ WINDFLOWER

VALLEYFIELD ■

Quebec.

St Lawrence

Halifax. ■ESQUIMALT
■CLAYOQUOT
OTTER

New York

ASPECTS OF CANADIAN NAVAL OPERATION
SECOND WORLD WAR

Legend — Solid black circles show positions of German U-boats destroyed by Canadian
forces; participating ships are named. Inverted triangles show Italian submarines
destroyed. A cross surrounded by a circle shows the position of U-boats destroyed by
R.C.N. and Allied forces; only Canadian ships are named. The squares show the last
known position of Canadian warships lost, 1939-1945.